Good
Intentions Are
Not Enough

Why We Fail at Helping Others

Good Intentions Are Not Enough

Why We Fail at Helping Others

Robin Low
Civil Innovation Lab

WS Professional

NEW JERSEY · LONDON · SINGAPORE · BEIJING · SHANGHAI · HONG KONG · TAIPEI · CHENNAI · TOKYO

Published by

WS Professional, an imprint of
World Scientific Publishing Co. Pte. Ltd.
5 Toh Tuck Link, Singapore 596224
USA office: 27 Warren Street, Suite 401-402, Hackensack, NJ 07601
UK office: 57 Shelton Street, Covent Garden, London WC2H 9HE

National Library Board, Singapore Cataloguing-in-Publication Data
Name(s): Low, Robin, author.
Title: Good intentions are not enough : why we fail at helping others / Robin Low.
Description: Singapore : World Scientific Publishing Co. Pte. Ltd., 2016.
Identifier(s): OCN 958963351 | ISBN 978-981-32-0057-9 (paperback) |
    ISBN 978-981-32-0056-2 (hardcover)
Subject(s): LCSH: Philanthropists – Singapore -- Biography | Social service – Singapore |
    Humanitarianism.
Classification: DDC 361.74092 --dc23

On the cover: Border crossing at Dajabón market, Dominican Republic. Located on the border with Haiti. © Robin Low.

Desk Editor: Shreya Gopi

Typeset by Stallion Press
Email: enquiries@stallionpress.com

About the Author

Robin Low is the co-founder of Civil Innovation Lab, promoting social impact through civil action and local innovation. The Lab runs in collaboration with various universities including Stanford University to enhance efficiency and impact on social initiatives.

He is also the principal consultant at the Patatas, advising corporations on CSR projects with real social impact, and promoting a new level of corporate/civil partnership to solve the world's pressing problems.

Robin co-founded Relief 2.0, which promotes sustainable disaster recovery, by engaging, empowering, enabling and connecting survivors to the support they need. His work has taken him to more than 20 countries, where he shares how arts and craft, for example, can help communities support one another in times of disaster. Robin is also working on the post-earthquake recovery of Nepal.

Robin owns Greenyarn LLC, a nanotechnology company based in Boston which manufactures sustainable socks, fabric and apparel for environmentally conscious consumers. He also founded Doing.gd, a social movement to help make volunteering and doing good easy, and is a mentor at Grameen Creative Labs.

Contents

Success is not about beating others, but the ability to contribute to a community.

Good intentions are not enough. It takes the right action, performed with the right consciousness, to produce the necessary results.

Sadhguru

Good intentions are not enough. You cannot tape the cracks of a sinking boat.

1. Introduction

Many people mean well and want to contribute solutions to local and global needs. People often want to act for the sake of "doing something". Often, this means poorly thought-out ideas that are often unsustainable, or have little measurable social impact. Are these efforts actually helping? Are they solving problems or creating new ones? What pitfalls should a concerned giver watch for?

I was in New York City in 2001. I went to the World Trade Center shortly after it collapsed and I've been involved in large scale disasters ever since. Initially, it was just volunteering for some of them, and working with charities and non-governmental organizations (NGOs) on the ground.

I am very passionate about new processes, ideas and technology. Getting involved in different businesses lets me continuously learn new skills and challenge myself in new tasks. When I started actively going to disaster areas, it allowed me to experience different communities in a harsh and extreme setting where decisions need to be made quickly and decisively. I do learn a lot from every experience, and what's more, the knowledge that you have impacted someone's life or saved a community of people makes your work there feel especially important, much more than anything else that you do day to day.

In 2008, I had various business setbacks. My father passed away and I had various bills to pay along with a foreclosure. Many of my companies were affected and my rich friends and business partners avoided me. It was a painful experience to sell away a lot of what I owned, walking away from a big property investment and terminating my rental lease in various countries.

My gamer friends and academic friends were very supportive and helped me readjust to a new lifestyle where I had more time to do what I enjoy doing, and focused less on making money just to pay for my large expenses.

With more time, I could also examine a lot of my life choices and ask many questions, as well as search for answers. At this time, I found many new passions which I got involved in, and one of them was social entrepreneurship. It felt like a brilliant idea where you can do good while make money, and I thought to myself, "Why is everyone not doing this?"

Rich People are Not the Solution

I've known many rich people who do not consider themselves rich. These people I know live in properties that cost in excess of US$25 million, run foundations or own businesses, and continue to generate a lot of income. Through my interactions with them, I have realized that most of them still have a lot of anxieties — anxieties relating to financial security.

Often, when I approach these people who run foundations, I've candidly asked them why they don't do more for society personally, and I get the same answer all the time: "You know, the costs of education and necessities are getting more day by day, my businesses may be doing well now, but who knows what is going to happen tomorrow?" Sometimes, I do get puzzled as the small projects that I wish to be funded are under $10,000, and their response of financial insecurity in their Rolls Royce prompted me to follow up with another question: "So how much do you need to have in order to be financially secure?" The quick answer is often "$1 billion in the bank."

Many people talk about doing social good, creating social impact, and many of them have the means to do it. Some who run foundations will get their foundation to be involved, but foundations usually do not spend time on small-scale prototypes, and many rich people do not seem to be financially secure enough to part with some money.

I've met public servants earning more than US$1 million dollars a year, refusing to support an educational project for local youths and who pointed me to government grants which either take too long to apply for, or simply are not the right match.

If you are in the business of fund-raising, you often get this common reply: "I'll donate more next time when I have more money." Boston College did a study on the Fears of the Super Rich, and found that even people with an average net worth of US$78 million are dissatisfied with their sizable fortunes.[1]

So if you think that you will donate only when you are rich, the question you should ask yourself is, how much money do you need before you can consider yourself rich?

---

[1] http://www.theatlantic.com/magazine/archive/2011/04/secret-fears-of-the-super-rich/308419/

Social Enterprises — Really that Social?

When Social Entrepreneurship came along as a new and shiny concept , many people jumped on board. Many entrepreneurs like the idea of creating business that does good at the same time. Fundamentally, the very concept of a social enterprise is flawed. Companies pay taxes, and the taxes go to schools and roads. So, does that make all companies social enterprises? What's more, when examining these concepts in practice, flaws are even further exposed. At the bottom of the social needs pyramid, the needs of people are more basic and less varied.

Poorer communities need basics like food, shelter and clean water. If you can sell to meet the needs of one community, you can also sell to others. As such, many enterprises that sell to one poor community will try to scale-up and sell to others. However, when a startup scales, it runs into problems. It can lose its ability to be nimble. It can become bureaucratic, and communication with the ground level can suffer. Social projects that scale too quickly often fail. When scaled too quickly, many social enterprises which may have seen success in the small scale may even lose their social impact and cause social harm.

Microfinance is a good social idea that allows poor people to have basic financial services. Recipients of microfinance could start a small business and are less likely to pull their kids out of school due to economic reasons. However, many people take the simple idea of giving loans to the poor and twist it to make it very profitable. Payday lenders are getting popular in many poorer parts of the country and each year, about 12 million Americans incur long-term debt by taking out a short-term loan that is intended to cover borrowers' expenses until they receive their next paycheck. This causes many people to slip out of the middle class. Some of the lower income borrowers may pay up to 400% per annum in interest rates, causing up to 40% of them to default and push them closer to poverty.[2]

I am a serial entrepreneur and in my experience starting many companies and working on countless projects, I've experienced many failures which I've learned a lot from — some of them could have even be avoided if I had listened to advice.

I feel that the redistribution of resources is a very pressing issue that needs to be solved. Resource is definitely limited and especially for projects trying to help marginalized families, any waste of resource is detrimental to the efforts of making things better. I have volunteered and run many different projects in different

[2] http://www.microfinancegateway.org/sites/default/files/mfg-en-paper-us-microfinance-at-the-crossroads-scale-and-sustainability-can-lessons-from-international-experience-help-guide-the-us-sector-sep-2012.pdf

countries trying to address pressing problems, and have failed. Sometimes I do not even know that my actions did not have any social impact on the ground. Just the feeling of doing good makes me feel better inside, but on having it pointed out to me, I then realize that it was a waste of resource and effort.

Many people want to do good. Some want to help one person at a time, and others want to change the world. Helping one person at a time creates intimacy, but some fear that the blunder may get personal, and even when it succeeds, it does not change anything in the big picture. Trying to change the world may be ambitious, cleaner and more abstract. But success is distant and unlikely, so people who attempt this often taste a noble failure.

I've met many people and learnt from many mentors, some even younger than me, trying to do good. Learning from their experience, models and failures, I realize that many people may not know the best way of doing good. Some do it because of their religions; others may like the feeling of helping someone. Everyone has their reasons. As I look at the result of their project, I realize that many people doing the same thing and getting the same results may come up with different conclusion of success or failure. Nevertheless, what matters most is the real impact of the effort. Is it moving in the right direction?

I have worked on many projects in the past 15 years. It is interesting to me that my perspective has changed in these years, and some projects which I've considered a success in the past, are failures to me now. My failures taught me a lot, and even if I cannot convince you about what you should do, let me at least share what not to do.

Doing Good

In doing good, there is no "best way". Doing something is often better than doing nothing. However, the result may vary depending on actions. Instead of saving a drowning boy in a shallow pond, for example, what if the clothes you would have soiled, had you jumped into the pond, could be sold for more money to donate to a charity that would save more than one boy? There are always options to weigh before you take your action. There may be no right or wrong. I can only share my opinions, experience and insight, in the hope that they can give you more options when it is your time to do good.

A person who is far away, whom you cannot see or hear, and with whom you have no memories or loyalties in common, cannot compel your help in the same

4

way as a person right in front of you, or in some sense one of your own. Ignoring the cries of a drowning child would feel like a violation of the most basic kind of compassion; anyone who did it may seem less than human. However, cultivating sympathy for unseen and unknown people seems to be simply abstract, admirable, and "more than required of an ordinary person".

Take for instance two similar disasters in different countries. I find it harder to garner support a country like Nepal — fewer people have personal or business connections or a physical or emotional connection causing them to care. On the other hand, it is easier to get support for Japan, where people may have Japanese classmates, colleagues and friends, or watch Japanese anime and own Japanese products, even though the country may already have the capacity to recover from the disaster.

To most people, the distance between themselves and another person — both physical as well as emotional — has a profound effect on their sense of duty. Many people want to do good or be seen as doing good, but may believe that if it was their duty to save one child, then why not five children — why not five thousand?

The fact is that most people would rather think up excuses for their behaviors of inaction, than find ways in which they can contribute in their current capacity. Supporting marginalized communities does not necessarily mean donations or volunteering, there could be other innovative ways to connect or engage the community which may lead to greater impact. Unfortunately, most people prefer to stay in their comfort zone, thinking of excuses.

For the few that want to make a difference, I admire their courage to step out and take action. In some cases, their actions do create much social impact for the community, and in other cases, the impact may be minimal. Bureaucracy and other reasons may be blamed, and again, the easy action is then to complain.

This book is not a guide on how to do good, but rather, a sharing of my experience on why complaining and maintaining status quo does not solve the most pressing of problems. For those who care and want to do more, they should focus on testing new solutions that will solve the problem. With the advancement of technology, there are a lot of problems which can be solved with new knowledge and tools.

There are also a lot more problems created with a bigger human population, and it is not enough if we do nothing. Humans are capable of doing terrible things, but humans are able to do heroic things that inspire as well. There is just one thing to remember, all heroes or saints were normal humans until they decided to take actions which set them apart.

2. Shifting Morals and Ethics

Comparison Chart

	Ethics	Morals
What are they?	Morals are concerned with the principles of right and wrong behavior and the goodness or badness of human character	Ethics are practical, conceived as shared principles promoting fairness in social and business interactions
Origin	Greek word "ethos" meaning "character"	Latin word "mos" meaning "custom"
Where do they come from?	Social System — External	Individual — Internal
Why do we do it?	Society accepts it	We believe it is right
How flexible are we?	They tend to be consistent within a certain context, but can vary between contexts. Largely dependent on the surroundings and others.	Mostly consistent, but change when an individual's beliefs change, due to more knowledge gained or personal experience
How is it accepted?	Ethics are governed by professional and legal guidelines within a particular time and place. Largely dependent on culture	Morality transcends cultural norms

Conflict between Ethical versus Legal

"Legal" is an adjective and a noun used to describe anything that concerns the law or its workings. It is associated with all equipment, processes, procedures, practices, languages, cultures, and other relative concepts in the system of the law.

In many situations, the relationship between the law and ethics clashes yet works. Many existing laws have originated from ethics, and in turn come from the perception of rightness or wrongness of an act or conduct. There are some instances where legal acts can be unethical and others where ethical acts are considered illegal. It all depends on the current governing laws and perceptions of the people in the act as well as outside of the act.

The Death Penalty in some countries may seem unethical to many people, but it is definitely legal. At the same time, it is illegal for doctors to administer euthanasia in many countries, even when there is no cure, and prolonging the life of the patient only leads to more suffering.

Conflicts between Ethics and Morals

Stem cell research offers hope that could save millions of lives, but it requires the destruction of human embryos. The researcher may believe it is morally right, but his religion questions his ethics.

A lawyer may feel that murder is morally wrong, but his business ethics tell him to defend his client to the best of his abilities.

Ethics, Morals and Laws Change

What is acceptable today may not be acceptable tomorrow. There are shifts in the limits of ethical acceptability over time, stemming from advances in technology, change in cultures and beliefs or just a better understanding of science.

When ethics change over time, what you know about what is acceptable changes as well, however, your mindset may not have adjusted to the changes. This does not mean there are no shifts in the limits of ethical acceptability.

Ethics guide us on what is right and what is wrong, and ethics change because situations change. It hard to judge if the way things were done in the past is right or wrong, without looking first at the context.

So were people unethical before women's suffrage?

Even today, women are not allowed to drive in Saudi Arabia. Before you judge, you need to consider culture and context.

The Bible gives instructions on how slaves should be treated (Deuteronomy 15:12-15; Ephesians 6:9; Colossians 4:1), but does not outlaw slavery. In Biblical times, slavery was socially acceptable. But it was practiced very differently from the slavery that was practiced in the past few centuries in many parts of the world. Slavery in the Bible was not based exclusively on race. In Biblical times, slavery was based on economics; it was a matter of social status. People sold themselves as slaves when they could not pay their debts or provide for their families. In New Testament times, sometimes doctors, lawyers, and even politicians were slaves to others. Some people actually chose to be slaves so as to have all their needs provided for by their masters.

Ethics change with time and technology. In the medical field, the advancement of science does challenge and shift our ethics. Even today, organ transplantation is a controversial topic, the guidelines and policies are still changing. There is a long list of people who need organ transplants. Is it ethical to choose not to donate your organs when you die?

Emerging technology is pushing the limits of our ethics and regulations. Just like organ transplantation, now stem cell research, tracing genetic roots and genetic modification are creating debates on ethics and safety. The development of the research is strongly dependent on social acceptance which cannot escape public scrutiny and regulation backlash.

Emergent Artificial Intelligence (AI) which is widely used in speech and recognition will be used in more robotics. Revolutionary developments in AI and the computational power of current computers will see more use in autonomous vehicles. In the near future, AIs and robots may also perform simple medical procedures, fly drones, drive cars and even repair and adapt themselves without maintenance.

Smart pharmacology will permit us to use antidepressants and neuroenhancers when our dopamine level drops and our emotions will be controlled by smart machines. Nanomachines will be in our blood, repairing cells and fighting cancerous cells. What is the ethical consequence of such developments that may make us less human and more dependent on technology to survive?

How will people 20 years in the future view us — a society which still largely relies on the fossil fuels that caused all the weather problems which they are facing? With newer sustainable technologies, will their values on using fossil fuels change?

Morals change over time. How have our views on the following subjects changed in the past 10 years?

- Homosexuals
- Drugs
- Other Religions
- Other Races
- Swearing
- Cross Dressing
- Transvestites
- Transsexuals

- Co-habitation

- Interracial Marriage

- Sex outside Marriage

- Open Relationships

Moral Acceptability: Changes Over Time

% Morally acceptable

	2001 %	2015 %	Change (pct. pts.)
Gay or lesbian relations	40	63	23
Having a baby outside of marriage*	45	61	16
Sex between an unmarried man and woman	53	68	15
Divorce	59	71	12
Medical research using stem cells obtained from human embryos*	52	64	12
Polygamy (when a married person has more than one spouse at the same time)**	7	16	9
Cloning humans	7	15	8
Doctor-assisted suicide	49	56	7
Suicide	13	19	6
Gambling**	63	67	4
Abortion	42	45	3
Cloning animals	31	34	3
Buying and wearing clothing made of animal fur	60	61	1
Married men and women having an affair	7	8	1
The death penalty	63	60	−3
Medical testing on animals	65	56	−9

Note: Sorted by change in the percentage saying each is "morally acceptable"; unless otherwise marked, issues first measured in 2001
* First measured in 2002
** First measured in 2003

GALLUP

Values (Ethics) also change over time:

- Slavery

- Birth Control

- Universal Suffrage (Women's Rights)

- Immigration
- The Hippocratic Oath (Abortion, Confidentiality, For Benefit of Patients)
- Euthanasia
- Atheism
- Cloning
- Genetic Screening
- Genetically Modified Food
- Role of Authority
- Public View on some Roles (Teacher, Doctors, Parents)

Law and Ethics cannot keep up with technology.

Discrimination can happen easily with algorithms that seek specific types of people, and judge people from their social media feeds. What will happen when a self-driving car has a software failure and hits a pedestrian, or a drone's camera happens to catch someone naked taking a shower, or a robot kills a human in self-defense?

As science and technology advance, the laws and our ethics are challenged. To feed billions of people on earth, to prolong the lives of the elderly and for our convenience to do things faster and more efficiently, the new changes that we need to adapt to may not be socially acceptable. Soon, with 3D printing, cloning, and advances in artificial intelligence, more change will come and our ethics will be further challenged.

It is hard to judge whether some of these new technologies are right or wrong, as we have not even come to realize their full potential, and the cultural norms or ethics that may be challenged in the progress.

3. Why We Fail at Helping

Charities and non-profits have been around for many years and charities seem to get bigger with record donations received almost every year. Yet, the problem of poverty seems to be getting worse.

There are many attempts at making charities more efficient after complains about how the bulk of money donated to the non-profits is going towards administrative costs and not to the beneficiaries. Some people think that applying for-profit business management techniques and using business matrices to measure efficiency is a good idea, but sometimes, it does cause other issues.

> Example:
>
> I have seen a few ground-up organizations doing good work running schools which provide meals for the kids at the school and clean water for the parents to take home. When there are calls for reports and accountability, to compare the organizations, the schools that are in the villages cost more to run. When you add in transportation cost, the schools in the city — being more accessible — tend to cost much less to run.
>
> In some reports, the schools in the villages can easily cost four to five times more to run per child, and most of the cost is due to logistics. The further the school, the greater the need for the food and education, but the higher the cost.

Unfortunately, many donors who call for transparency and accountability just compare the numbers out of convenience, and will donate to the schools in the city. As a result of the convenience of donors, most of the schools in the cities get more funding and the schools in the villages, which need more, get less funding.

Such discrepancies not only apply to schools. After a disaster happens, the outpouring of International Aid usually stays in the city, where multiple organizations will support the same survivors who have already received aid from other organizations. The villages which have been hit harder by the disasters tend to receive aid much slower as they are usually inaccessible due to poor infrastructure.

People today want to rely on statistics and figures to tell them how to donate. In many cases, statistics provide an idea of how an organization is run. However, many companies and organizations can easily use the data to their favor, to mislead people or say a lot of nothing.

Averages

The average of *1, 2, 3, 4, 5* is 3, right in the middle.

The average of *1, 2, 3, 4, 40* is 10, which does not give you an idea of the bigger picture.

"Fastest Growing Organization"

Having statistics to show that you doubled the number of beneficiaries and are the fastest growing organization look very impressive.

However, in some cases, growing from two beneficiaries to ten beneficiaries does not create a vast increase in social impact, but it does show a growth of 500%. On the other hand, between one organization which manages 400 refugees and a second one that manages 600 refugees, it appears to be only a 50% difference, but the logistics requirements and the need for fundraising increase tremendously.

Cost of Running an Orphanage for One Year (in dollars)

	Organization A (40 children)	Organization B (400 children)
Food	100,000	2,000,000
Admin	50,000	500,000
Expenses	50,000	500,000
Education	100,000	1,000,000
Cost per child	7,500	10,000
% Spent on children	66.6%	75%

The data above can be used in many ways to market each orphanage to their advantage.

Organization A seems to be more cost efficient, even though it is a smaller organization. The running cost to keep a child in the orphanage is $7,500 per year.

Organization B, however, only uses 25% of the funds for Administration and Expenses; 75% of the funds are used for the children.

The numbers do not show the quality of care for the children, the nutrition of the food or the standard of education, all of which may matter more than the data showing the numbers.

As you can see, there are many ways to interpret statistics to show what you want to tell, without even talking about what is most important — how does it benefit the children?

We like to support initiatives which are brought to our attention. When you buy a pair of shoes from Toms Shoes, the company will donate a pair of shoes to an underprivileged child. This is a for-profit company which solves shoelessness, but it hardly has any effect on poverty.

We do what is convenient to us. We pray for the people who were massacred by gun violence in the U.S.; we "like" some posts on Facebook; we donate $5 to charity to feed a poor family. Have we thought about whether our actions had any real impact on what they intend to support, besides making us feel good about ourselves?

So does "helping" at our convenience cause any harm?

Recently, I was involved in the Nepal Earthquake recovery. In almost all disasters, there is a high chance that blankets given out by church groups will contain a bible inside. I have seen this in many different disasters, and I have no problem with it as the recipients in Nepal actually used the bible for fuel when necessary.

I've spoken to many church groups about their intention of spreading faith during disaster relief and recovery, and I get the same response all the time: "If they have lost their bible in the disaster, we want to provide them with one so they can pray." However, I still feel that a bible in every blanket they deliver is a little excessive in a country where the majority of the locals are Hindu or Buddhist.

The blankets are much needed, especially in the higher altitudes where the survivors still live in tents one year after the earthquake, and temperatures can drop very low.

However, a group of volunteers delivering blankets decided to do it at their convenience. Instead of taking the blankets to the villages that most needed the blankets, they visited tents in Kathmandu, where they distributed the blankets. Most of the survivors have no use for the bible found in their blankets, so the bibles were discarded, and when the government found the pile of discarded books, they asked around and found out about the bibles in the blankets.

As religion is a sensitive topic for most governments, this has caused the government to increase its bureaucracy on volunteers. All aid to be delivered needs to be inspected and taxes to be paid. Volunteers and organizations need to be registered and their aid declared; undeclared aid can be charged as smuggling.

A simple convenience for delivering aid can create inconvenience for everyone else. Whether it is volunteering or donating, we do what is convenient for us. We give and volunteer without thinking about the impact caused.

An oversupply of doctor volunteer can create unemployed doctors, too many volunteers or foreign contractors coming to rebuild homes can affect local contractors from getting hired. In many instances, international donations have to be spent in the country it was fundraised in, resulting in the importation of building materials and foreign labor, neither of which benefit the local economy of the disaster area, and in many cases, the locals are excluded from the rebuilding process.

Operating in Silos

Large organizations have economies of scale, funding and infrastructure. However, many of these organizations fail to deliver sustainable social impact. Organizations that feed marginalized people may know that their work is just going to be harder as more people fall into poverty, and even when the ones engaging with the recipients know the ground and situation well, the management and other departments do not know what is going on.

Like large corporations, many different departments operate in silos. Customer-facing departments don't talk to one another. Marketing doesn't talk to product development, web teams don't talk to customer service, and consultants don't have access to key stakeholders or executives. The advertising teams don't talk to public relations. User Experience doesn't talk to product development.

The dangers of operating in silos are plenty. In charities and non-profit organizations, these inefficiencies will see much duplication in efforts to do the same thing, and what's worse, the actual needed change is not communicated to the other departments — they will only find out when a crisis happens.

When the operations team engages with recipients of aid, they build trust and get a lot of feedback. However, when the feedback is lost in the poor communication within the organization, the trust can quickly be eroded and alienation may occur.

I have observed several water projects that provide clean water to rural communities. When one of the concerns — managing the waste plastic bags which are not recycled and cannot be disposed easily — was not communicated with the Research & Development (R&D) team, the newer products actually had more plastic parts which were made lighter, cheaper, but ended up creating more waste. The waste clogs up the ecosystem after years of operation, and it takes a news report on the effects of the plastic waste to be shared and become a social media crisis, before the organization tries to act and change. But by then, much of the trust is lost and the communities stop using their products and have searched for alternatives.

For social enterprises, the challenges are much greater when there is scale. To make things worse, the silos created will result in inconsistency, which may break the organization apart. When a social enterprise gets funding from a source that wants a return on investment, the profits that the enterprise makes going back to the funder may be in conflict with the interests of the people who support the social enterprise.

Office Politics and Bureaucracy

In large organizations, this politics and bureaucracy are also big problems, preventing real work from being done. Bureaucracy makes large organizations react slowly to change, but many forward-thinking organizations now do form and work in teams to solve problems regardless of position and job scope, and this has largely helped in solving urgent issues.

4. Traveling Overseas to Help? Whom are You Helping?

"Voluntourism" is getting popular, but there are many ways to smell foul. All over the internet, you can find articles about how ineffective short-term voluntourism trips to developing nations are, but many people still engage in them.

I have been guilty of volunteering for some NGOs to organize some of these trips, and after visiting the location and looking at the actual activities the volunteers will do, I was appalled.

Yes, I'm talking about the short trips where professionals or students visit Nairobi to build orphanages, and up with a short trip to Rift Valley taking photos with the wildlife to prove it. There are too many examples where people visit Haiti to build schools, or visit communities in the rural communities in Latin America to teach English for a few days, and end up visiting exotic sites.

Even in local communities, people with the best intentions may visit orphanages or mentally challenged children, but after bonding with a child, their leaving may sometimes cause more harm to the child's psychological growth. And when you bring such good intentions overseas, some organizations do exploit the people or communities they pretend to help and ending up doing more harm than good.

The idea of service learning is good, doing meaningful community service with instructions and reflection can enrich the learning experience. However, many people are ill-prepared and lack the necessary tools to be effective. Yet they would like to believe that their presence (not their money) would make a lifelong difference in a child's life.

A common response after doing a voluntourism trip is: "I was heartbroken to see how life is there. It really makes me realize just how good we have it. My life will never be the same." Many popular voluntourism trips cost a lot of money and are essentially self-fulfillment trips. It is about "you" and your experience, and giving you a different perspective. Let us not call it humanitarian work when the only person that benefits from it is "you".[3]

---

[3] http://qz.com/665764/instagrams-white-savior-barbie-neatly-captures-whats-wrong-with-voluntourism-in-africa/

As reported in Al Jazeera America, "As admirably altruistic as it sounds, the problem with voluntourism is its singular focus on the volunteer's quest for experience, as opposed to the recipient community's actual needs."[4]

Calling a Spade — A Spade

Tourism does help the local economy, and the locals in that community do benefit in some form or other. After a disaster, visiting the disaster country, using local services, and buying local products do help the local economy. Go because the country is interesting, but do not call it altruism.

> Don't go on exploitative trips that are out to make money. If the trip sounds too good to be true and is entirely focused on your needs, chances are it will be about the tourist, not about the community. Check if the organization you travel with is about the community or about the volunteers. Some organizations that offer short stays may have good impact with the community and are catalysts for good.

Most short term trips have limited impact. I've been to an orphanage in Sri Lanka which is said to house orphans from the Asian Tsunami in 2004. I've seen volunteers teach the kids English, give the kids bracelets and stationery items, and leave thinking they have changed the lives of the kids. In reality, the kids don't care and play along because they get school uniforms, food and basic healthcare when they come to the schools, but the lessons learnt the previous day are often forgotten.

Sadly, this is not even the worst case I've seen as one of my Sri Lankan friends pointed out that some orphanages are just schools, and that the kids are from the nearby villages. It must be a profitable industry to sit around, receiving funds while visitors do all the training.

Orphanage Tourism is harmful to children.[5] Many of the children already suffer from abandonment issues, yet people visit slums, orphanages to have photo opportunities with the kids just to share their deeds on Facebook or social media. These children don't need pity temporary attention or to be someone's model for the day; they need solutions that can provide long-term access to education, food, healthcare and medical treatment.

---

[4] http://america.aljazeera.com/opinions/2014/4/volunter-tourismwhitevoluntouristsafricaaidsorphans.html
[5] https://www.youtube.com/watch?v=oziNspf9OwM

Traveling overseas to feel better about one's lives when one sees people suffer is more or less schadenfreude — enjoyment derived from others' troubles. It is also an incredible waste of money. I've seen doctors with Doctors without Borders visiting Haiti after the earthquake, and in the same area, you can see other doctors from Christian organizations and NGOs. In fact, there are so many doctors in the area that local clinics and hospitals have closed down.

Many of these doctors spend thousands of dollars to visit and volunteer, taking the jobs away from local doctors, and foregoing income by being in Haiti. A better approach would be interviewing a local Haitian doctor who has been displaced, and paying him a working salary to do the same thing a volunteer would, except that the local doctor can speak the native language and knows the local culture better.

People may get the impression from organizations that organize projects to build homes that accountants and doctors can build homes for people living in poverty. However, there is a big difference between skilled labor and unskilled labor. Most volunteers are unskilled and there are limited things they can do, yet they pay a premium to feel good about it.

Voluntourism create a cycle of dependence. When volunteers give out free food and services, local farms and business are impacted and cannot survive. Locals do not have jobs and have to rely on aid to get by. Aid in Africa is in fact a contributing factor as to why they still require foreign aid and why the local economy is getting worse.

Food for thought: Many people hate people from third-world countries stealing their jobs, but accepting lower salaries. Is your volunteering destroying opportunities for a local to be hired, and who can do it better than you, because the cost of hiring you is ZERO?

There are also instances where there can be direct harm caused by voluntourism. I've been to homes where there are autistic orphans who bond with some of these volunteers, and I have seen an orphan go into emotional withdrawal and depression when the newly-bonded friends leave. The orphan became withdrawn and shunned all other social interaction.

When the next batch of voluntourists arrived, it now took longer for the orphan to bond, but the emotional trauma became worse at the departure of every group The orphan just stopped eating and went into a deep depression. A few months later when I checked with the home on the status on the orphan, they informed me that he was no longer with us.

In Nepal, after the earthquake, groups of students from Singapore arrived and they volunteered in various projects. As it is compulsory for students to clock "Community Involvement" hours, many of them choose to go overseas for a holiday and to be "involved in projects".

Contrary to their understanding of construction of being a low-skilled job, building a stable building is not easy. Making a flat layer upon which they lay cinder blocks and mixing your own cement is not a simple task and should be supervised by someone who knows construction, preferably, a civil engineer.

In Singapore, students ask for permission for everything, but they don't seem to do so when overseas. A group of Singapore volunteers actually raised funds and built an elementary school themselves. It was clear that the building was not well built as the cement mix was bad and the bricks did not line up, and shortly after the volunteers left, the building collapsed, hurting some children.

Of course, the student volunteers do not see this as their problem and do not accept any accountability, and the organizer will simply deny and ignore the event as it did not happen in their country.

Sadly, there is money to be made, and voluntourism will continue.

5. Scapegoating

It is normal for people to push blame to others, especially when there are voiceless persons.

Scapegoating is the practice of singling out any party for unmerited negative treatment or blame. Scapegoating may be conducted by individuals against individuals (e.g., "he did it, not me!"), individuals against groups (e.g., "I couldn't see anything because of all the tall people"), groups against individuals (e.g., "Jane was the reason our team didn't win"), and groups against groups.

For many years, donations have been the default model to help people living in poverty. Nothing much has changed to improve the lives of the recipients of aid, and the recipients are often blamed for it.

Many social enterprises give jobs to people from marginalized communities. Some of them pay only minimum wage, and others who hire the elderly or disabled may only hire them part-time, denying them benefits. There is also often no progression in the jobs, and when these people leave the job, they are frequently blamed for not sticking to the job.

Without engagement, many NGOs and governments try to think of solutions to help these communities. And the communities are told to be grateful and to just accept what is given to them. The solution may not work as often, foreign experts are used and no consultation is done, and there is also very little buy-in from the community. When the project fails, the communities are blamed for the failure.

6. The Dangers of Social Intervention

When we help, we make life decisions for people we try help. When they succeed, we claim credit, when they fail, we blame them for not trying or not following instructions.

When we help, we feel content to help but fail to see the whole picture.

We search for the approach most efficient for us and not those we are trying to help.

We exclude those we are trying to help from making decisions.

We displace local capacity.

We measure success by the delivery of help or completion of actions and not actual impact.

For foreign donors, much of the donations remain outside the relief area and end up getting spent in their own countries.

We help out of pity.

From my experience in going to many disasters, I have seen many things not done right. I have volunteered with several big organizations and have seen some problems with the current disaster relief model.

Together with Carlos Miranda Levy, I set up Relief 2.0 — with the practice of running the last mile in the field in disaster response through independent field units supported by mobile technologies and social networks, connecting resources, stakeholders, needs, organizations, volunteers and survivors in an efficient, effective and timely manner, filling the gaps created by bureaucracy and slow response from top-down hierarchies.

After the Haiti Earthquake, Carlos decided to provide aid to the survivors. After much planning and connecting with other like-minded people, Carlos managed

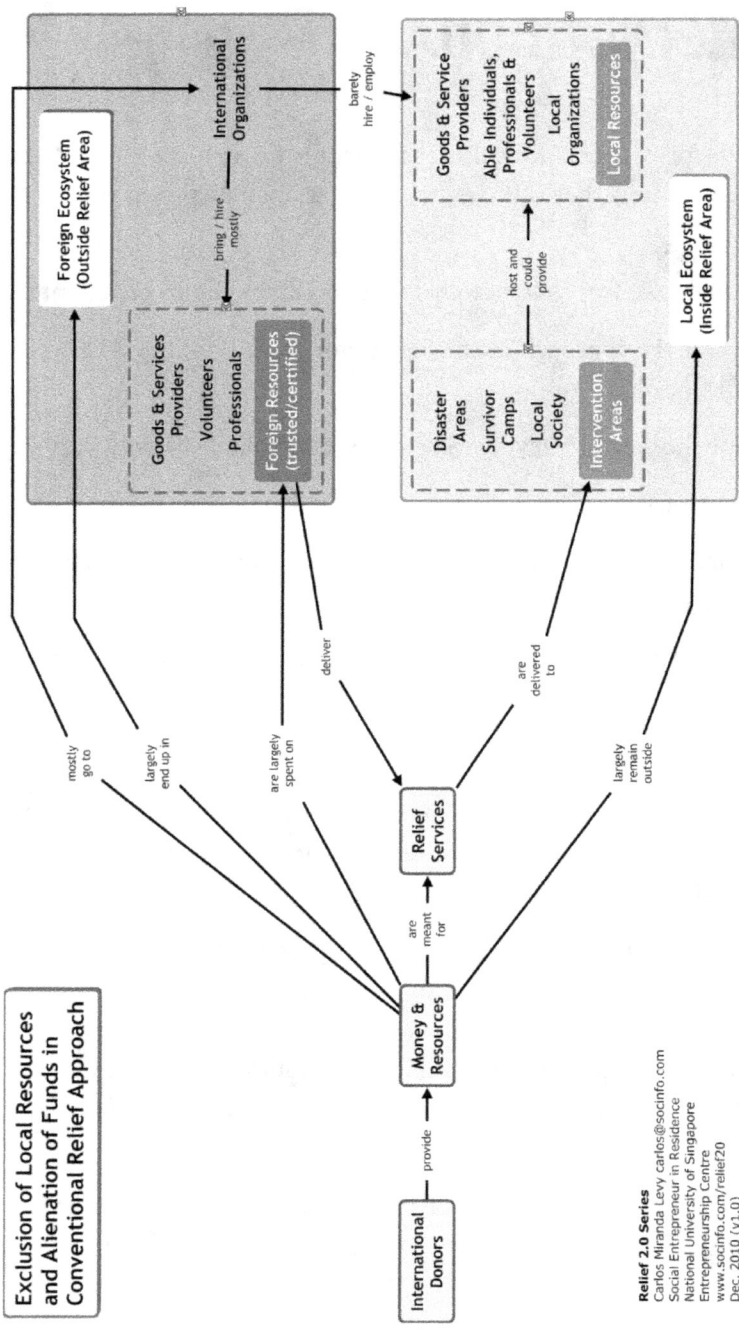

Exclusion of Local Resources and Alienation of Funds in Conventional Relief Approach

Foreign Ecosystem (Outside Relief Area)

International Organizations

bring / hire mostly

Goods & Services
Providers
Volunteers
Professionals

Foreign Resources (trusted/certified)

barely hire / employ

Goods & Service
Providers
Able Individuals,
Professionals &
Volunteers
Local
Organizations

Local Resources

host and could provide

Disaster
Areas
Survivor
Camps
Local
Society

Intervention Areas

Local Ecosystem (Inside Relief Area)

deliver

are delivered to

largely remain outside

mostly go to

largely end up in

are largely spent on

Relief Services

are meant for

Money & Resources

provide

International Donors

Relief 2.0 Series
Carlos Miranda Levy Carlos@socinfo.com
Social Entrepreneur in Residence
National University of Singapore
Entrepreneurship Centre
www.socinfo.com/relief20
Dec. 2010 (v1.0)

Image by Carlos Miranda Levy

22

to get a lot of aid to send to Port-au-Prince to support the much-needed logistics there.

Hiring a truck and driving over the border from the Dominican Republic, Carlos provided aid to many survivors and supporting the relief organizations with aid stuck at the airport customs, the supplies were much needed. This is how anyone would have done it and everyone felt good.

When Carlos was talking to a young girl in the tent city, though, there was a shocking revelation.

Young Girl: "Is the driver Dominican?"

Carlos: "Yes, why?"

Young Girl: "Are there no drivers in Haiti?"

Carlos: "…"

Young Girl: "Can't Haitians drive?"

Carlos: "…"

Even after my numerous experiences at disaster areas, it never occurred to me that we could source for a local driver who can do the same job and could use the money to rebuild his home. It took a six-year-old to point that out to me. Needless to say, we immediately tried to hire a Haitian driver and truck for our further deliveries.

After Haiti, I started to see the curse of exclusion in every disaster area. From Japan to Philippines to Nepal, non-local volunteers flood the disaster area providing the much-needed support. The intention is great and it is heartwarming to see the outpouring of aid and support, however, it is also disturbing that locals are put in shelters with barbed wires and are often excluded in the relief efforts.

Reflection

My experiences in visiting disaster areas did not change my views greatly until that incident in Haiti, which made me think deeper into the current practices. Just because it is the way we do things, it does not mean that it is the right way.

In every disaster, who are these survivors in the shelters?

By engaging them, you get to know that they are teachers, doctors, engineers and much more. Disasters may destroy the physical infrastructure, but the social infrastructure remains. Just because there is an earthquake, it does not mean all the survivors have lost their skills and knowledge. A doctor is still a doctor, a carpenter still a carpenter.

7. The Curse of Exclusion

There is much evidence that has shown that depression overcomes many survivors in the shelters when they have lost everything and have everything done for them. Helplessness sets in when they feel that even simple tasks such as cooking are being done for them. There are a lot of benefits to empowering survivors to participate in the relief and recovery, yet in most cases, they are being excluded.

The rebuilding process and planning is rarely done with any inputs from people living in the shelters, even though it is their homes and town that are being rebuilt.

While I do believe that NGOs are doing a good job providing shelter and food after a disaster, I feel that in many cases, volunteers can come from the shelters and these survivors can be engaged and consulted in the recovery of their own towns.

The curse of exclusion does not only apply to post-disaster recovery. In fact, this happens in many other cases when we fail to engage while we are trying to help a community.

Even in Massachusetts, the urban renewal projects aimed to create a better environment in the poorer neighborhoods use labor from other cities. In areas with unemployment and public housing, the state had some funds to widen the roads and rebuild some public schools. However, none of the labor used in these urban areas consisted of locals. The same poor people this project is supposed to benefit are not given jobs when they applied for them, and the unions got the contracts. In some areas, the community fought for the locals to be part of the labor and after much protest, they managed to get the city to make the contractors hire local workers.

Whom does urban renewal benefit?

It is a known fact that the gentrification pushes out the poor community. Most of the poor people rent their homes or live in public housing. They work locally in low wage jobs and have barely enough to get by.

When the neighborhood gets more developed, residential rents go up, more expensive "quirky" stores open as there is more street lighting and parking space, and the commercial rents go up. Food gets more expensive, the landlords may renovate their homes and residential rents go up further, making it unaffordable for the poor to stay.

This disruption not only causes the poor to lose their jobs as it is too expensive to travel from their lower cost areas to the now "nicer" part of town; their children may also not go to school as it may now be too far away.

The end result usually sees a lot more middle-income people move to the area, and fewer lower-income people remaining, rather than the lower-income sector getting more opportunities to move to middle-income earners.

Why is there a curse of exclusion?

When I ask this question to non-profit organizations, the general answers I get are:

"The locals are corrupt and we don't know where money will go when we give money to the locals in the rebuilding project."

"The locals are not looking for such jobs, it's also hard to find someone with the skills we need."

"The locals are unreliable and unprofessional. When we pay them, they will not show up the next day."

These answers are strange, because from my experience working with the locals, most of them genuinely want to have jobs to rebuild their homes. When you pay them during the progress of getting the job done, there is very little risk of default. As you may know, when locals are hired, the money remains in the community which needs it most, and they get to decide how to use it.

My friend Anna Blume suggested that locals need to be deeply involved in solving problems as many problems are growing increasingly challenging. If it would be a general practice for local communities to be consulted and included in the problem solving process, it would be a wonderful tool for value creation.

Transparency and dialogue are keys to building trust, and for complex problems, communities need to be empowered to work on solutions and take ownership. One complex problem that communities should come together to solve is climate change, which affects many countries already. The discussions can be a springboard for deep change in the communities.

The Spectrum of Community Engagement

INCREASING IMPACT ON DECISION-MAKING

INFORMING	CONSULTING	INVOLVING	COLLABORATING	EMPOWERING
Providing balanced and objective information about new programs or services, and about the reasons for choosing them. Providing updates during implementation.	Inviting feedback on alternatives, analyses, and decisions related to new programs or services. Letting people know how their feedback has influenced program decisions.	Working with community members to ensure that their aspirations and concerns are considered at every stage of planning and decision-making. Letting people know how their involvement has influenced program decisions.	Enabling community members to participate in every aspect of planning and decision-making for new programs or services.	Giving community members sole decision-making authority over new programs or services, and allowing professionals to serve only in consultative and supportive roles.

Adapted from the IAP2 Public Participation Spectrum, developed by the International Association for Public Participation.

Note: Engagement activities can include community surveys, neighborhood outreach projects, partnerships with grassroots organizations, public meetings, and efforts to select community representatives.

Source: The Stanford Social Innovation Review (Available at: http://ssir.org/articles/entry/community_engagement_matters_now_more_than_ever)

8. Paradox in the Social Sphere

When people give out of pity, they tend to create dependence and a mindset that the rich should give and the poor should just receive. Donors think they are better than the recipient, and want to be treated with respect, expecting that others should view their deed with high regard.

However, they feel offended when they see the poor spending money on something "luxurious" or when the poor are getting a better standard of living.

So rules are set up to restrict the poor from getting too much. Means testing (which costs more overheads and inefficiency) is set up because people do not like the poor to defeat the system, even when they know that the rich do this all the time.

Subsidy/Salary Gap

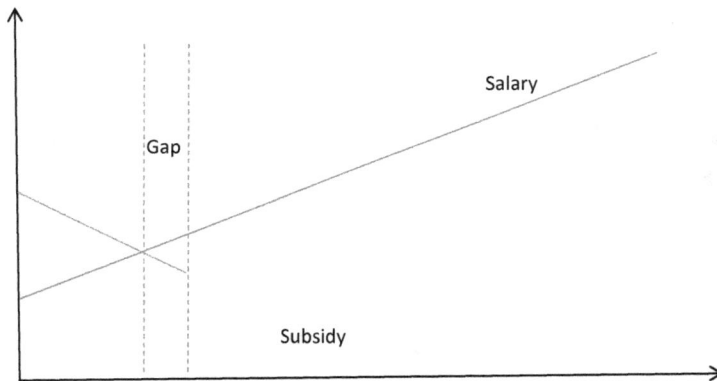

Gap: Because of the reduced subsidies, you end up with less than when you earn more.

Many of the rules are set up for the case where the recipients do not work. When some of these recipients start to improve themselves and start to earn an income, people think they do not deserve any further subsidies. For example, when the salary increases, the subsidies will decrease sharply and **the person may make less than when they were paid a lower salary.**

When the poor person finds a job and start to earn money, the rules kick in to reduce the amount of money they receive. For most of the time, these rules work and the poor can slowly support themselves without any subsidies as they progress and earn more.

However, in many scenarios, the recipient of aid gets kicked out of low-income housing and some healthcare plans if they earn above a certain figure. This arbitrary number is usually not enough for the recipient to rent an apartment and get their own healthcare plans. Hence, by working harder, they are penalized as they get less or lose their home. This will destroy ALL motivation to work hard to get out of poverty. This is mainly due to the fact that they CANNOT afford those benefits even with the increase in salary.

Working harder, getting a promotion and pay raise, but finding out you get a lot less at the end of the day just does not make sense.

Food Donations

When you donate food to end hunger, the food is usually imported and local farmers and workers lose their jobs because they cannot sell. Over the years, this impact causes more people who need food as they fall into poverty.

Lack of Investment in Agriculture

Too many developing countries lack key agricultural infrastructure, such as enough roads, warehouses and irrigation. The results are high transport costs, lack of storage facilities and unreliable water supplies.

All of these conspire to limit agricultural yields and access to food. Investments in improving land management, using water more efficiently and making more resistant seed types available can bring big improvements.

Research by the UN Food and Agriculture Organization shows that investment in agriculture is five times more effective in reducing poverty and hunger than investment in any other sector.[6]

More investment in "The Blue Economy" Projects would create more jobs, more income, more value to the soil and biocultural diversity.[7]

---

[6] http://www.fao.org/home/en/
[7] http://www.theblueeconomy.com

Food Wastage

One third of all food produced every year (1.3 billion tons) is never consumed. This food wastage represents a missed opportunity to improve global food security in a world where one in eight is hungry.

So Much Grain, So Many Hungry People

Some 70 to 80% of grain produced in the United States is fed to livestock. Half the water consumed in the U.S. is used to grow grain for cattle feed. The local people at the farms go hungry as these farmers do not grow enough food crops, and they have to import food.

Poor Farmers

In many third world countries, the farmers in villages only know traditional ways of farming. The yield is not good and with industrialization, pollution and climate change, the farmers generally don't have enough food to feed themselves.

Even in a good harvest, without a method of transporting the vegetables to the city, these farmers rely on middlemen who make most of the money, leaving them with little.

In many rural villages, these subsistence farmers find the situation getting worse in the villages, and the teenagers in the villages go to the city to look for better opportunities. This mass migration causes the population of the cities to grow fast, and salaries of jobs to remain low. This also causes inflation in rents and slums around the city, which in turn causes much pollution.

Without much opportunity in the cities or in the villages, these young people either turn to crime, vice or begging, and those with more means will leave the country as migrant unskilled labor to be exploited in other countries.

In China, with the growing of affluence, the consumption of meat has increased. China already buys more than 60% of the world's soybean exports to feed to its own livestock and has been a net importer of pork for the last five years.

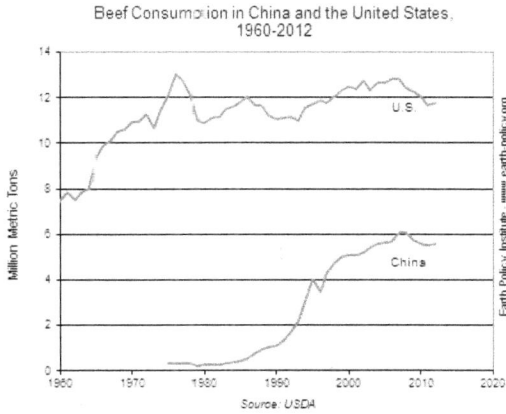

Beef Consumption in China and the United States, 1960-2012

Source: USDA

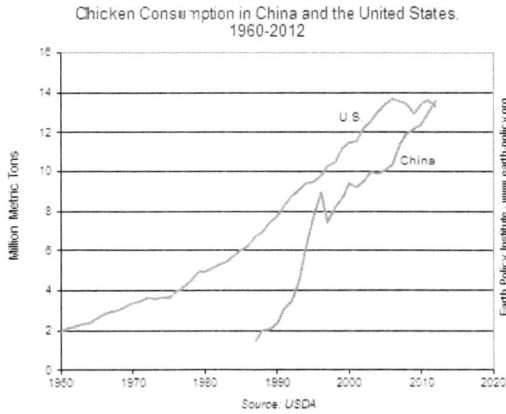

Chicken Consumption in China and the United States, 1960-2012

Source: USDA

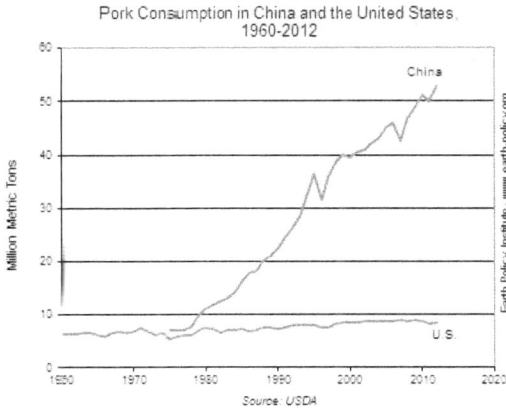

Pork Consumption in China and the United States, 1960-2012

Source: USDA

With the increase in affluence in countries like India and China, people consume more meat which requires more feed. Much of the current practice of farming today is still unsustainable. Water is diverted from rivers, making it harder for rural farmers to feed themselves.

With pollution from factories, the industrial farmers have to use a lot of fertilizers and pesticides to get the yield they want, and the excess fertilizers and pesticides wash off in the rain and go into the rivers, further polluting the water.

The lives and the futures of these farmers do not look good. Instead of finding ways to reduce pollution and fight climate change, we help them by giving them aid. To provide aid to more people, the clothes and food we source are the cheapest ones we can find. By choosing the lowest cost products, we encourage these business that pollute to produce more and hence pollute more. This will just perpetuate the cycle and make the poor farmers more dependent on aid.

While the rich nations promote an increase in production of "cash crops" such as fruits, vegetables, grains, many poor farmers themselves go hungry. Meanwhile, much of the wealthy world protects its own farming sector and subsidizes its agribusinesses making it hard for the poor countries to compete fairly.

Over the world, large scale deforestation is executed to create land to farm. Even with more farming land, people remain hungry. This is mainly due to the fact that these farms are used to grow non-food crops.

In the South America, the large-scale Amazon rainforest is converted for ranching and increasingly to grow soybeans. In Indonesia, the rainforests are burnt down to grow oil palms. Palm oil is used surprisingly in many of our daily products. The forest is, by and large, not being cleared to feed the hungry.

These developing countries may see many people getting out of poverty, but the conditions of many others will certainly become worse. The current model of capitalism drives unequal distribution of resources to a point where the poor will be dependent on aid. Charities do not address the uneven playing field, and the people with resources seem to want to keep it that way.

Free/Subsidized Housing

When people with the best of intentions build subsidized housing, free schools and offer jobs, millions will move in. If there is not enough money as the aid is only intended for thousands, there will be slums created, schools will be overcrowded and there will be not enough jobs. Eventually, the education standard will be poor, living conditions bad, and jobs scarce — leading to more poverty.

If we believe that trade is important, we could do more to open our own markets to trade from developing countries. If we believe property rights are important, we could do more to enforce the principle that nations, not illegitimate leaders, own their own natural resources.... If we believe transparency is important, we could start by requiring our own companies to publish the details of the payments they make to developing countries.

This is seen in many developed countries as well, like rich families owning everything, creating monopolies and unfair advantage as they can influence government to create laws which favor them.

— *Owen Barder, a senior fellow at the Center for Global Development*

Free Mosquito Nets

Angelina Jolie and a few other famous artists gave out more than one million mosquito nets to fight malaria, destroying the entire local industry of mosquito net makers and repairs. Many who could pay for mosquito net repair decide to just use the new ones, which put local manufacturers and repairers out of jobs.

More Food ≠ Better Nutrition

There are many projects where people are given better food and more protein (subsidized diets projects). In many cases, the recipients who save some money on food do not use the protein to subsidize their diets, but decide to make it their sole food,, and spend the money saved on cigarettes.

Unequal Perception Triggers Wrong Innovation

When a neighboring village gets a clean water project and other benefits because they are identified as living with polluted water, many other villages will soon intentionally have polluted water, because they may be smart enough to see that having polluted waters may result in them having drinking water that is cleaner than what they originally had, and for free.

Funding does not Fund Results

In many cases, funding is spent on the doing. Many people like donating to initiatives to fix cleft lips, give stationery items to students, or deworm children.

The funding for such initiatives can be massive enough to impact millions, yet there will be no funding given to investigate reports whether doing such initiatives could reduce poverty, build capacity or give the kids a brighter future. No tests, no accountability, no results.

Overheads to Run a Charity Well are Seen as "Inefficient"

Most of the time, NGOs are compared based on total percentage of donations delivered to beneficiaries. However, they are not measured by quality of service rendered, or transparency and detailed reporting. Many NGOs pay their staff very little, and provide bad service.

A soup kitchen using 60% of donations for free food may be seen as a worse soup kitchen than one using 80% of donations for free food. But here are the numbers:

Kitchen 1	Kitchen 2
$10,000,000 donations per year	$200,000 donations per year
$2,000,000 for Auditing, Administration, Infrastructure and Salaries	$30,000 for Salaries
$2,000,000 for Marketing and Fundraising	$10,000 for Marketing and Administration

Kitchen 1

- Quality campaigns and events are run to engage donors;
- Donors can visit and communicate with recipients directly;
- Quarterly reports are given
- 2,000 beneficiaries served.

Kitchen 2

- Not much awareness created;
- Run by volunteers;
- No reports or accountability;
- 30 beneficiaries served.

With just some numbers, it is hard to compare charities as numbers do not show the whole picture. Numbers tell part of the story.

Kitchen 3	Kitchen 4
$10,000,000 donations per year	$100,000 donations per year
$2,000,000 Auditing, Administration infrastructure and salaries	$5,000 for Salaries
$2,000,000 Marketing and fundraising	$5,000 for Marketing and Administrative

Non-profits need to be audited and to have offices. Regardless of size, they will have overheads. Smaller NGOs have less overheads. However, being small can hurt their credibility. Numbers only tell part of this story. Consider two other soup kitchens, 3 and 4. Kitchen 3 spends $0.60 per dollar raised on the program (soup). The other spends $0.90 per dollar raised. However, Kitchen 3 employs professional staff that prepare food safely and with low waste. The other uses volunteers who are less skilled. Yet, evaluating by overheads is easy to do, and doesn't require additional work. Bigger programs need infrastructure, staff, and more insurance. They will always have higher administrative costs than an outfit run by a charismatic leader who attracts volunteers.

Success, Scale, Fail

This phenomenon is seen in many projects, whether in entrepreneurship or social impact initiatives The skill sets required to run a startup and to run an enterprise are very different. Without the ability to delegate, many founders of these companies will fail to scale.

Through a lean startup, many people are able to run a simple model to verify their assumptions and test their ideas, and once proven successful, some are able to get funding to scale up. In many cases, the idea of "think big, scale fast" is the root cause of these failures.

When a venture capitalist (VC) or a large foundation provides a big grant, they expect results fast. Hence the implementation is done without further testing and is based upon the initial prototype. In many cases, the scaling might be done in other communities rather than the prototype community, and the situation would be different. Due to a lack of understanding of these other communities that they wish to operate in, the assumptions taken in the implementation — that may have worked with the prototype — may fail. With testing and firefighting taking place at multiple sites at the same time, catastrophic failures are inevitable.

Irony of Earth Hour

One billion people will participate in "Earth Hour", an annual global event, by turning off their lights from 8:30-9:30pm. Earth Hour is an event where people who want to spend some time for the environment and against global warming show their support by switching off the lights.

The premise of saving energy is good. Hypothetically, switching off the lights for an hour would cut CO_2 emissions from power plants around the world. However, many appliances in the house are still turned on: refrigerators, air conditioning, televisions, computers. So power plants will still have a large load even though the load is slightly reduced. Power plants will still continue to supply the same amount of power as the lights will turn back on in an hour, so there is actually no reduction in emissions.

Many people however, still want to have some form of illumination during Earth Hour, and they do so by lighting candles or turning on flashlights. Hence, there is actually more CO_2 produced during earth hour.[8]

Many people would like to "do something simple" like donating, or switching off the lights for an hour, and not think about the consequences of their actions. Many people like participating in awareness campaigns and sometimes doing something symbolic for the sake of "doing", but which actually has absolutely no social impact at all. This vain symbolism reveals exactly what is wrong with today's feel-good activism.

---

[8] http://www.slate.com/articles/health_and_science/project_syndicate/2013/03/earth_hour_is_all_wrong_we_need_more_electricity_not_less.html

9. The Great Convergence[9]

The Divorce and Remarriage of the Arts and Sciences and How Business Decided to Grow a Heart: A Reflective Thesis

Robert E. Brown (Harvard Professor, Communications)

In the seventeenth century a dissociation of sensibility set in, from which we have never recovered.

Eliot, 1921, p. 121

The rising profile of the social entrepreneur on the global stage is among the most compelling phenomena in the marketplace of ideas. What I have chosen to do is to offer a series of reflections on a dimension of social entrepreneurship from the margins. Those dimension the long and frequently bitter rivalry between what could be understood as the heart and mind that comprise the body of the concept of social entrepreneurship.

My thesis, if these reflections can be called a thesis, is that the heart and mind of social entrepreneurship and its creative intellectual innovators can be understood through the filter of the long and frequently bitter rivalry between the arts and humanities and the sciences. A word of caution: This thesis does not amount to conflating "mind" with the sciences or "heart" with the arts and humanities. What is intended here is what is meant by the idea of a *sensibility*, which is, simply put, a perspective, a way of seeing, hearing and responding.

By tracing the development of the rivalry between the sciences and the humanities and arts, the profile of the social entrepreneur can be understood not in terms of simplistic *deus machina* heroism, but as a figure and a concept which has a long, contested, annealing development. For social entrepreneurs are not only products of their time, but of millennia of intellectual history.

Three limitations of this thesis must be registered up front. First, in the relatively short space of a chapter, the reflective thesis begins merely four centuries ago,

---

[9] Brown's paper highlights the converging nature of things and the importance of thinking in terms of the big picture, as well as working collaboratively, rather than in silos.

rather than where it might well have begun — with the pre-Socratics. Second, the thesis must acknowledge the limitations of an American scholar's perspective. Third, the sensibility of the thesis author has its source in an eclectic background in corporate communications, the arts, and the social sciences. Such a combination will inevitably strike readers in two distinct ways: as either more or less than the sum of its parts.

The reflective thesis begins with, and returns to, the metaphor of a troubled marriage.

Background: The Great Disruption

The marriage — or, more precisely, remarriage — is occurring half a millennium from the divorce. Announcement of the divorce arrived around a century ago with the force of one of Western literature's most innovative literary artists, the poet, T.S. Eliot. When Mr. Eliot issued his finding, he had yet to become what he was to become: the unofficial dean of poetry, the arts and humanities.

Just who were the parties divorcing? That's where the plot thickens. It would be tempting to identify them as Science and the Humanities. Or the Technorati and the Literati. But while these are the contemporary avatars of the ancient pair, these are not the divorcees to which Mr. Eliot was referring in his twentieth-century essay, an essay whose singular pronouncement would develop a life of its very own. No. The original divorce was, if you will grant me yet another metaphorical source, rather like the biological splitting of a single cell — that cell being what Eliot called *sensibility*, and whose agents were the greatest poets of the Renaissance.

This dissociation of sensibility — remember that it is less a theory than what humanists like to call an insight — was signaled by what Eliot believed to be a synaptic gap between the extremely odd approach of the "metaphysical poets" of the late sixteenth and seventeenth century — John Donne, most prominently — and the great poets of the middle ages and Renaissance until that split — Dante, the best known among them.

But at the risk of betraying this famously, notoriously complex insight (or opinion, if you prefer), let me venture a simpler explanation before proceeding directly to the main portion of this chapter, which focuses on the era of great convergences.

Put simply, Mr. Eliot had hit upon a brilliant defense of his own radical and (to use a contemporary coinage) disruptive aesthetic. For, like the radical disruptive poets who were scolded as *metaphysical* by the decorous Enlightenment author Samuel Johnson, Mr. Eliot was himself a disrupter:

> Let us go then, you and I,
>
> When the evening is spread out against the sky
>
> Like a patient etherized upon a table (Eliot, 1970a, p. 13)

Etherized? *Really?* Comparing the lovely poetic evening to a poor sap on a gurney?

And:

> I should have been a pair of ragged claws
>
> Scuttling across the floors of silent seas. (Eliot, 1970b, p. 15)
>
> Comparing the fellow to a crab? Really? Is that quite kosher for poetry?

But, then, back in that dissociative synaptic gap, the great English poet, John Donne, had already raised the disruptive ante:

> Our eye-beams twisted, and did thread Our eyes upon one double string.

In Donne's historically disruptive metaphor, lovers didn't merely gaze.

Their gaze itself materialized. The soul embodied!

Finally, this: What Mr. Eliot was defending was nothing less than modernity itself; himself, among the leading modernist artists of his era.

Foreground: The Great Convergence

Fast forward from the Middle Ages to the Renaissance to Modernity to where we are today: in the post-industrial, globalized, postmodern era.

The sea change of our digital and social-media era is history's C-change. Individuals, organizations formerly separate and distinct have either merged or are merging. Data and voice. Headquarters and franchise. Marketing, PR and advertising. Our RL (real lives) and our virtual lives. Offline and online.

A full accounting of the convergence phenomenon would far exceed the scope of this chapter. Such an accounting would have to recognize convergence across a multitude of contexts — political, economic, social, technological and otherwise.

While gesturing in the direction of the entire constellation of convergences that has come to signify this period of history itself, I shall concern myself to identifying those convergences that are exerting an effect on what I will call the communications industries, practices, and practitioners themselves.

That said, it will become evident that such a limitation may be rather difficult to maintain for the very reason that an era of convergence is, on its face, an era of radical expansiveness, inclusiveness and connectedness. I can cite here the technologically anthropological observation of Brian Solis, a principal of the San Francisco-based marketing and tech-trend-consulting firm called The Altimeter Group. Solis, who is among the most followed thinkers on the disruptive and opportunistic impacts of emergent technologies on business organizations, has highlighted the critical importance of the demographic he calls Generation C (connected). Styling himself a digital anthropologist, Solis has a knack for putting matters technological in dramatic, even apocalyptic, terms for the consumption of worried marketing organizations. His coinage of "digital Darwinism" gives the flavor of his portrait of the extinction that awaits businesses that fail to grasp and embrace the tech tools and strategic realities required to avoid losing credibility with Gen C, the "connected Generation" of consumers.

Background: The Marital Argument

I mean Negative Capability, that is when man is capable of being in uncertainties, Mysteries, doubts, without any irritable reaching after fact and reason.

— John Keats (Keats, p. 261)

Was Mr. Eliot right? Did the seventeenth century mark the divorce of the arts from the sciences?

To believe that, you'd have to accept the route Eliot took to arrive at his pronouncement. While it is safe to say that our contemporaries would agree that science — what scientists think about, do and how they do it — is far from unimaginable to artists, it must be admitted that artists and scientists draw upon rather different vocabularies. It is important to recognize, however, that science has always inspired art, an inspiration that continues. Consider how the aesthetics of the famous image of the great blue planet earth the early astronauts beamed back to us in all its holistic, pastel majesty inspired countless artistic creations — beamed back not by artists but astronauts. Artists, like astronauts and the rest of us, are (in Keats's phrase) "half in love" with the image and the awesome adventure into the unknown.

Mr. Eliot meets Mr. Keats. Their lives separated by a century. Both men of letters. Poets. Thinkers. Artists, unquestionably. Neither one would have referred to himself as a scientist. Why is that?

Both offered a famous speculation. Eliot's was the famous 'dissociation of sensibility.' Keats was infuriated by a friend's unimaginative literalism. For Eliot, the twentieth-century Modernist, the root of the problem — more than sensibility or mathematics — was language. The dissociation he landed upon was, tellingly, not between art and science, but within art, itself. For Keats, the nineteenth century Romantic, his irritation came from the zeitgeist: the Romantic No! to the Enlightenment's great Yes! Put succinctly by the Enlightenment poet Alexander Pope:

And, spite of pride, in erring reason's spite,

One truth is clear: Whatever is, is right.

(Pope, 1825, p. 19).

The Romantic poet warned that "philosophy" (by which he apparently intended Sir Isaac Newton's science) would "Unweave a rainbow." In the heyday of English poetic Romanticism, Mary Shelley, the poet Percy Shelley's wife, imagined a dystopia created by science in the still-famous figure of the monster of Dr. Frankenstein.

The world is familiar with David Bowie's "Ground Control to Major Tom" and Elton John's hip and gloomy "Mars ain't the place to raise your kids." One would not have to look far for examples of "high art" — painting, sculpture, libretto, symphony — or the marriage of high art with popular art, as in Stanley Kubrick's choice of a Strauss waltz to wordlessly, musically narrate a space ship's balletic approach to a slowly spinning space station framed against a canvas as black as a Rothko.

But what are we talking about here? These artists are inspired, no less than scientists themselves, by the astonishing beauty, terror, and mystery of the universe, the earth, and humanity. Shakespeare's Prospero, in "The Tempest," celebrated it famously and, indeed, with Romanticism two centuries before Keats's Grecian urn and three before W.B Yeats's Byzantium:

> O brave new world, that has such people in it. (Shakespeare, 1936, The Tempest, V, i)

Eliot's 'dissociation' ought not be taken literally, though it is fair enough to understand it technically as a matter of language, and occupationally as a matter of focus, and methodologically as the difference between the codified scientific method and the artistic spectrum from systematic to chaotic.

On the eve of World War II the poet W.H. Auden was anxious. But his concerns worsened considerably in years immediately following the war's end. In a magazine article he confided that he feared the atomic bomb.

But we may be surprised at the source of his fear.

> Not, of course, any military use of it, but I read somewhere a suggestion that a possible peacetime use of the bomb would be for breaking up ice-caps. If this devilish scheme were ever to be carried out, I shall indeed be sunk, for my Isofjorthur might easily acquire the climate — a fate worse than death — of Washington, D.C.
>
> (Auden, *House and Garden*, 1947, p. 336)

[As for Auden's reference to Isofjorthur, Iceland, the city is reported to enjoy a temperate climate.] A half century before the projections of apocalyptic global warming, the English poet imagined, with characteristically sardonic wit, a scenario implicating the atomic age in a scenario of climate change.

The Two-cultures Quarrel

In 1933, in the decade after T.S. Eliot's marital report of the irreconcilable differences between the arts and sciences, the old argument flared up with new combatants. It was called the Leavis-Snow controversy over "two cultures," now mostly forgotten. What irked the eminent literature professor Leavis, an Oxford don, was that C.P. Snow, an English chemist, had argued, in a high-profile public lecture, that there existed a "gulf of incomprehension" between scientists and "literary intellectuals" [more broadly, with the humanities, we would say today].

Leavis struck back at what he regarded as philistine condescension; Snow held his ground. The battle raged in the journals. (Snow, 1959)

The consensus is that 2003 got the better of the argument. Leavis emerged looking like an angry reactionary whose rage underscored Snow's case that science welcomed the future, while the arts and humanities dug their heels into the past. It was generally believed that it wasn't the scientists who were unable to comprehend the literati, but the other way around.

Twenty-first Century: Sunset of the Literati

… on a spring afternoon of the year 2000 … that was when I began to notice people on the streets of Tokyo staring into their mobile phones.

— Howard Rheingold (2003, p. xi)

When I was a freshman at the Bronx High School of Science, one of New York City's elite public "exam" schools, I found myself called into the gym with my fellow students for what was advanced as an important announcement by the school's principal. The announcement: even for a school famous for its special, challenging preparation of students in science and math, there would be yet more science and yet more math.

The source of this was the of the space race, that competition between the U.S. and the Soviet Union to be first — first in space (they were: Sputnik I, 1957), first to put a man in space (Yuri Gagarin, 1961), first to land on the moon. The moon race eluded the Soviets when, in the summer of 1969, the American astronaut Neil Armstrong landed on the moon and took his famous "one step for man, one giant leap for mankind."

Science was sexy then. It has become sexy once again, although computer and web Mark Zuckerberg and Steve Jobs have replaced Neil Armstrong and his fellow astronauts as role models in the sciences. In America, students are passionately encouraged by all the forces of influence — parental, financial and otherwise — to embrace STEM: science, technology, engineering, and math. By contrast, the status and reputation of a course of study in the arts and humanities — and to some extent the "soft" (social) sciences — has been so thoroughly downgraded that the downward path has led to these same arts and humanities seeking to transform and rebrand themselves in new analytical and critical methodologies such as the "digital humanities."

There are two striking differences between the helmeted, space-suited astronauts and the jeans-and-tee tech icons, one compelling similarity. The differences are about the level of risk and the significance of compensation. Astronauts were soldiers who were perpetually risking, and sometimes losing their lives. As the author Tom Wolfe portrayed them, the defining quality of the astronaut was having "the right stuff," not the million-dollar compensation or the public stock offering. In a sense, the astronaut's mission was the explorer's quest; the tech icon's has been the entrepreneur's domination.

But what the astronaut shares with the tech billionaire is not the *s* in STEM, but the *t* — less about the science itself than the tools; not theory but gadgetry. Technology, like business, is measured and rated and promoted and funded by results that can be seen and quantified. Technology, in this sense, is a zero-sum game. What excites the partisans of STEM to invest in a STEM curriculum is very different than what excited the astronauts to orbit the earth. The result of a social-media platform reaching its millionth end-user is light years from the result of an astronaut jumping from his space capsule platform onto the surface of the moon.

STEM, the new paradigm of higher education in the twenty-first century, has replaced the old paradigm of a liberal education, and the nonpareil in that latter quartet isn't science but technology. It makes economic and financial sense. Science can be monetized but technology is money. Tech is the star player; the other three are but supporting players. Silicon Valley billionaires, not white-coated lab scientists or mathematicians or engineers, grace the hagiographic covers of *Fortune*, *Forbes* and *Business Week*.

Web 2.0 — Dawn of the NeoLiterati

Remarriage is the triumph of hope over experience.

— *Samuel Johnson*

Digital media have revolutionized the practice of scholarship from the archive to the monograph. Over the next few decades, computation will become as vital in humanistic scholarship as it is today in fields like plasma physics and climate modeling. Researchers have already begun to develop new methods for analyzing online collections which are too large for traditional methods, and students now require formal experience with digital technologies to be competitive, both in academia and other workplaces. (Princeton, 2013).

Perhaps there was no such divorce, no such "dissociation of sensibility" as Mr. Eliot had purported to identify and trace to the sixteenth and seventeenth centuries, and to pronounce the source to be — of all people — poets.

Or perhaps Mr. Eliot was on to something. After all, his pronouncement was hardly more than common knowledge. Science and the arts do not speak the same language. David Bowie, Lady Gaga and the Off-Broadway theater may be inspired by the astronomical image of black holes, quarks and the expanding universe. But it would be the rather unusual artist who can explain the concept in detail, much less have the slightest notion of how to read the mathematical language upon which rests those inspiring concepts and images.

But if these are the pragmatics of a dissociation, there is a kind of physics that, in the twenty-first century has been a powerful force in the equal and opposite direction of a re-association.

In the technology industries, voice and data are converging.

In education, the humanities have collided with digitization.

In international affairs, official state diplomacy has comingled with unofficial "public" (read: private-citizen) diplomacy.

In business, marketing has been integrated with public relations and comingled with advertising, and taken up with a fourth partner: politics, which itself has merged into entertainment.

In romantic adventures, personal introductions have been traded off for on-screen swipes.

On my person, my mobile device has been clipped to my belt.

In my experience, what's real has moved ever closer to what's *virtual.*

My finger is a phone, my brain an operating system, my life a searchable database.

Marriage Counseling

The occurrence of remarriage, if it is to be a success, is typically predicated on the divorced parties having undergone a period of re-negotiation. The twenty-first century's information and communication revolution has resulted in the triumph of technology, which is the embodiment of science most visibly in things — mobile devices, driverless cars — but also in thinking, in personal, social, national and organizational values, in behaviors, in public opinion, and in business. The most financially valuable company in America is not Exxon or General Motors, but Apple. The most powerful and personal relationship individuals have with a product is no longer with their automobile but their mobile device. Millennials' affiliation with technology is mirrored in their dis-affiliation with automobiles.

The distinction between science and technology is a crucial one in terms of attitude, opinion and behavior. What the Romantic poet John Keats objected to was different from the imaginative terrors of his wife, Mary Shelley, the author of *Frankenstein.* The poet was repelled by the prospect that science's project was, as he feared, to "unweave the rainbow." But Mrs. Shelley's dystopic novel has had a lasting and powerful impact because she envisioned a dramatic scenario beyond the abstract threat of science and embodied it as the huge and malevolent monster. It is merely a quibble that the dreadful monster has been portrayed in movie versions as misunderstood, hunted, and even sympathetic. He's still a monster.

Philosophically speaking, Mary Shelley was a consequentialist utilitarian, and the Frankenstein's monster she envisioned placed science itself in the background and technology in the foreground. Fast-forward from the early nineteenth century to our own, and Mary Shelley's dystopia has been upended. In the postmodern world, technology has been rebranded as the ultimate and only visionary solution to all the crises facing humanity — from climate change, to medicine and healthcare, to business and economics, to romantic relations, to the politics of democracy, to education, and finally to the understanding of consciousness and the self.

In the wake of the technological transformation, other transformations are occurring. Boundaries, once relatively apparent, have been crossed or blurred. Most of these boundary-crossings, transformations and replacements are by now familiar. In the communications industries, the traditional distinction between marketing, advertising and public relations, for example, has been all but subsumed by their mutual embrace of digital communication, visuality, entertainment, and reliance of social media. In higher education, the "sage on the stage" has been replaced by screens projecting TED Talks and online classes without physical classrooms. In the academy's departments of literature and the humanities, the "digital humanities" are the rising tide. The reputation and status of employees across the organizational spectrum is increasingly the product of the perception of their adoption, grasp and application of technology. In organizational and social life, texting has replaced email which had replaced voicemail. Romance and dating behavior has been rendered quaint by the visualization and screen-swipe decision-making enabled by apps. In American political campaigns, the politics is polling.

The Heart of Business

A century and a half ago, in the shock of the post-Darwinian age, the English poet Matthew Arnold wrote an anthem of spiritual depression called "Dover Beach" in which appear these lines, which struck me fifty years ago as a Senior in high school:

The Sea of Faith

Was once, too, at the full, and round earth's shore

Lay like the folds of a bright girdle furled.

But now I only hear

Its melancholy, long, withdrawing roar (Arnold, 1867)

What depressed Arnold about the implications of the "withdrawing" of religion expressed the inchoate expressions of millions of others whose models of reality and meaning were a God-centric universe, much as their ancestors were horrified, enraged and puzzled by Copernicus's replacement of an earth-centered to a helio-centered solar system. Like Darwin's natural world, the social world was no garden, but a violent, competitive jungle red in tooth and claw. And it was this metaphorical map of the world that formed beliefs and values of those nineteenth-century American transcendentalists, as well as socialist and communist theorists for whom business itself was, according to their antipathies, a ruthless zero-sum game. Dispositionally unwilling to imagine that market mechanisms could serve as engines to lift millions out of poverty, the nineteenth century American romantic idealists and their socialist-theorist counterparts in Europe, asserted that in business there was no place for the heart or the soul. There's plenty of this sentiment in the novels of the most influential English author of century, Charles Dickens. The business model was a zero-sum game, an all-out war, a colonial exploitation, an imperial domination, a triumphant extinction. Such thinking, unfortunately, conflated the ambitions of colonial and imperial powers with the science of economics and the operations of actual businesses.

Such a philosophy obtained from after Darwin to the dawn of the social business, and it many quarters still holds sway. But by the middle of the twentieth century, in the aftermath of a pair of devastating world wars and the advent of the atomic age, it was becoming increasingly apparent that the post-Darwinian business model was, to coin a phrase, unsustainable. Depredations coming into stark view everywhere: in the fragility of the environment; in the instability of colonial regimes; in the extinction of innumerable species, and within the un-navigable stresses besetting the human body.

Relief had become a matter of desperation, and in desperation the West looked backward into history and Eastward to the religious and philosophical practices of Asia, where the model of the self and society was not the dualistic dissociation of mind and body but the holistic model of mind/body. This was a dissociation of a distinctly different order than the one the poet Eliot postulated, his being more narrowly drawn from his critical observations of seventeenth-century poetry, which persuaded him that in that century a crevasse had opened which had, for all times, split what had always been the holistic and unitary sensibility of the educated person into two incompatible sensibilities.

In America, such a radical notion, as previously noted, was the legacy of the nineteenth century movement called Transcendentalism, the intellectual movement led by Ralph Waldo Emerson, Margaret Fuller, Henry David Thoreau, Emily Dickinson and Walt Whitman. Part Germanic, part Asiatic, American transcendentalism interpenetrated eventually into the Human Resources models that have all but replaced the "personnel" departments of major American corporations. On corporate balance sheets, there arose the mission among leading companies of mid-century to go "beyond the bottom line." By the last third of the century, the concept of "corporate social responsibility" and "cause marketing" were no longer considered un-business-like, but had become the ethically legitimizing necessities of neo-liberal global corporate reality.

But even as this conscientious and cooperative business model had come to replace what a certain political class of Americans came to call the "tooth-and-claw" model of post-Darwinian capitalism, another, equally radical paradigm was being developed.

The Third Wave: The Social Entrepreneur

Poverty is created by deficiencies in the institutions we have built.

— Muhammad Yunus. (2011). *Building Social Business: The New Kind of Capitalism That Serves Humanity's Most Pressing Needs*. New York: Perseus Books.

By making a social mission the primary driving force of their enterprise, the social enterprise rekindles the concept of a remarriage of the arts and sciences.

Before the social entrepreneur was the philanthropist, a broad-brush approach high on aspiration and idealism and low on measurement and accountability. In industrial-age America of the late-nineteenth-to-early-twentieth centuries, iconic examples included steel millionaire Andrew Carnegie and oil millionaire John D. Rockefeller, Sr. it was an approach to business which would put a hero, not a system or strategy, at center stage. Philanthropy was, as the word derivation suggest, about the personal expression of an emotion (*phil*, or love). It was, in essence, a do-gooding — more top-down and one way, following the paternalistic values of its era.

A half-century after John D. Rockefeller's donations to medical research and an African-American college, came the wave of corporate social responsibility. CSR began, as I have argued, not as "giving-back" or even as a pro-active management strategy, but, initially as a vigorous crisis-response strategy intended to provide a robust defense by large oil and chemical companies based on the evidence of their responsibility for a variety of anti-social activities, from pollution to labor violations. Over time, this crisis management strategy developed into a proactive rebranding strategy whose adherents saw a shift to a more ethically sensitive and responsive corporate culture, while its critics lambasted as the way vice has forever paid tribute to virtue. Brown (2008) critiqued the pro-corporate narrative of corporate social responsibility as emanating from the simple desire of a company to "do well by doing good," theorizing that the real source of CSR was more likely the defensive crisis communication responses typical of environmentally problematic companies in the oil and chemical industry when a disaster such as an oil spill occurs as did in the Union Oil spill of 1969 in the Santa Barbara channel off the coast of pristine California.

Among the visible pioneers of CSR in the latter half of the twentieth century included Atlantic-Richfield Company, an oil-and-gas or "energy" company; Dayton-Hudson, a department store chain; and Borden, a food and beverage company. In contrast to the philanthropic movement, CSR moved away from the heroic individual expressing a personal emotion in financial and economic terms. Instead, CSR was the expression of corporate management, a collective, defensive and rebranding strategy whose ambitions included the controversial concept of going "below the bottom line." CSR was not a one-off. While less personal than philanthropy, CSR was intended to mediate the classic capitalistic motive with a menu of humanistic values — employee mental-health units; weight-loss gyms; scientific measurements of environmental impacts. Representative of that philosophy is a statement by the CEO of Dow Chemical Company in the 1980s:

> *If we have done a good job of meeting our social responsibilities, it is because we have been able to relate the profit motive to the solution of social problems, and, of equal importance (and driven by the same profit motive), to steer a course that has avoided conflict with the changing interests and concerns of society. (Orrefice, 1980, p. 197)*

What has followed in the tradition — or, if you prefer, the movement from philanthropy (the first wave of socially minded business) and CSR (the second wave) is the third wave: the social enterprise. CSR and its philosophic and operational cousin, *cause marketing*, moved the needle of the capitalistic enterprise from the economic and financial rigors of the classic for-profit, engineered efficiencies model of doing business. The social entrepreneurship, in its more visionary embodiments, has sought to reconceive the enterprise in terms that, while continuing to recognize inescapable economic and financial realities, place the emphasis elsewhere, primarily in social and cultural terms. The social business broadens the concept of costs beyond the classic rigors of the classical model's interpretation of success (profit, growth, return to investors). The social business redefines these terms by placing on an equal footing with traditional costs, environmental and social costs, while looking down the road to create the conditions that would be most likely to place the enterprise on solid economic and financial ground enabling it to sustain long-term sustainable growth consistent with pro-social values.

If philanthropy emphasized the personal heart; and CSR front-staged the collective ethic, the social business moves away from both the limitations of the individual and the organizational to a broader vision of the enterprise in more inclusivity, mutuality and social terms.

What distinguishes CSR from the social enterprise is what each makes primary and central to their mission. For CSR it's profit. For the social business it's sustainability. Companies practicing CSR have a traditional business focus on growth; for social businesses, growth in and of itself may even be problematic.

In the index to his book about the corporate ethos, David Whyte, an Associate Fellow at the Said School of Business at the University of Oxford, there are more than 40 references of "soul," more than 40 to "poems/poetry and "poets," and but three to "profits." In referring to business, Whyte, a published poet and business analyst, cites not only its softer sides but its "complexities" (p. 213):

> To remember what is good for our souls amid the complexities of corporate life, we must confront the shadows that fall over our work every day, and if there is any real shadow to the contemporary workday, it has to be that after centuries of pronouncements on the virtues of work we have together created a work world that attempts to reduce us every day to mindless worker bees. (p. 213)

It is one thing to speak of recalling the heart and soul as a palliative for the daily personal depredations of corporate life. But it has been quite another thing to do what the pioneers of the social business have done, which is to rethink, critique and move beyond the conventional interpretation of the immutable forces of capital markets to create a post-free-market framework of theory, values, and practice. This is precisely what Muhammad Yunus, a Nobel Laureate in Economics, has been creating and testing globally. In launching the microfinance practices of the Grameen Bank, for instance, Professor Yunus has neither rejected the realities and power of free-market capitalism nor neoliberal vision of globalization. Instead, he has reinterpreted these concepts by a methodology that moves the locus of economic and financial control from the semi-abstractions of large organizations and governments to the concrete and specific human locus of the individual entrepreneur. At the same time, Yunus and the social business model had replaced the goal of organizational profit with that organizational sustainability and social benefit at the center of the mission of the social enterprise, and capped that goal with the mission of ending global poverty — a mission well outside that of traditionally conceived enterprises of all kinds. It is the extraordinary ambitions of the social business that enable Yunus to classify it as a "new form of capitalism and a new kind of enterprise" (Yunus, 2010, p. vii).

While recognizing the power of governments to grow economies as their strength, social business sees government power and size as its weakness. Governments lack agility, move too slowly, push resources into the wrong hands, and are subject to corruption. Nonprofits, too, have proved inadequate to the task, as have foundations. In short, in framing poverty as the great and overwhelming crisis of the world; and in seeking to provide not simply a heartfelt, soulful, meditative palliative to provide a remedy for this crisis, innovative thinkers argue that social enterprise is the solution with the unique suite of strengths which make it the only business model capable of succeeding on both the local and universal stages.

The Great Convergence

Passage to India!

Lo, soul, for thee of tableaus twain,

I see, in one, the Suez Canal open'd,

I see the procession of steamships, the Empress Eugenie's leading the van;

I mark, from on desk, the strange landscape, the pure sky, the level sand in the distance;

I pass swiftly the picturesque groups, the workmen gather'd,

The giant dredging machines (Whitman, 1982, p. 532)

Call it romanticism, if you will, but the vision of Whitman's poem — and that of his entire career's poetics — was to bring together every disparate and disconnected part of the self and the world. For Whitman, the enterprise of the Suez Canal was a celebration of the essential oneness of all things, places, times, and peoples. Where T.S. Eliot saw an ineluctable divorce between the arts and sciences, Whitman saw a glorious marriage. Where Eliot would eventually come to embrace a Catholic faith as a remedy of personal healing, Whitman embraced the erotic and soulful nature of the body electric, and the unbroken thread of time and peoples everywhere, past, present and future.

No great result can come from less than a great ambition. Finally, what can be envisioned in the grand vision of the social enterprise is business's passage to more than India. The social business is the very model of a great ambition on the scale of a visionary aesthetic whose power derives from a vision which, at its heart, is about the marital convergence of the passion and intellect of the arts and sciences.

In the twenty-first century, it is the social entrepreneur who best embodies the great convergence — the marriage of the arts and sciences, of the soul and the body, of the self and society. For a coda, we grant the visionary poet the final words:

Passage to more than India!

O secret of the earth and sky!

(Whitman, p. 539)

References

Arnold, M. (1867). http://www.poetryfoundation.org/poems-and-poets/poems/detail/ 43588 Retrieved, May 6, 2016.

Auden, W.H. (1947). *House and Garden, [magazine], London*: p. 336.

Brown, R.E. (2008). Sea change: Santa Barbara and the eruption of corporate social responsibility. *Public Relations Review*, 34(4), 1–8.

Eliot, T. S. (1921, October). Review of metaphysical lyrics and poems of the seventeenth century: Donne to Butler, selected and edited, with an essay by Herbert J. C. Grierson. *Times Literary Supplement*.

_____. (1970a). *The complete poems and plays of T.S. Eliot*. London: Faber and Faber, p. 13.

_____. (1970b). *The complete poems and plays of T.S. Eliot*. London: Faber and Faber, p. 15.

Keats, J. (1959a). *Selected poems and letters*. Ed., D. Bush. Cambridge, MA: Houghton Mifflin Company.

_____. (1959b). "Lamia." p. 212–228.

Snow, C.P. (1959). The Rede Lecture. http://www.age-of-the-sage.org/scientist/snow_two_ cultures.html Retrieved, May 6, 2016.

Oreffice, P. (1980). In T. Bradshaw & D. Vogel (Eds.), *Corporations and their critics* New York, NY: McGraw-Hill.

Pope, A. (1825). *Essay on man. In four epistles*. Hartford, CT: Benton.

Princeton (2013). https://digitalhumanities.princeton.edu/new/ Retrieved, May 6, 2016.

Rheingold, H. (2003). *Smart mobs. The next social revolution*. NewYork: Basic Books.

Shakespeare. W. (1936). *The complete works of Shakespeare* (G. L. Kittredge, Ed.). Boston, MA: Ginn & Company.

Solis, B. (2014). http://www.briansolis.com/2014/08/orn-digital-meet-generation-c-new-generation-connected-customers/ Retrieved, May 6, 2016.

Whitman, W. (1982). *Whitman. Poetry and prose*. Ed., J. Kaplan. New York:Viking Press.

Whyte, D. (1996). *Poetry and the preservation of the soul in corporate America*. New York: Crown Books.

Yunus, M. (2010). *Building Social Business: The New Kind of Capitalism That Serves Humanity's Most Pressing Needs*. New York: Perseus Books.

10. Empowering State of Mind

Life is not fair, and fairness is not equality.

Equality is not always SOCIAL JUSTICE

This is EQUALITY   This is SOCIAL JUSTICE

Many people are obsessed with things they cannot control. Other people care about how others think about them. Many people feel jaded and believe that things have to be the way they are.

They are usually unhappy people who may be unpleasant to be with. They can bring your emotions down. They are always complaining, always blaming someone else and they never take actions to better the situation.

Instead of just focusing on problems that you cannot control, why not focus on what you can do?

When people are passionate about the things they do and work on solutions with people who want to help themselves, they form powerful communities which have the ability to affect change. These catalysts become leaders as people want to be around them.

So what does it take to be charismatic?

1) Optimism.

There is always an innovative solution to the situation. What is lacking may be resources, connections or simply the right attitude to move forward. A positive attitude is infectious and people get attracted to you, as a result of which, you do not have to handle the task alone.

In addition, as a community, you may have more access to the resources needed to succeed.

2) Inclusiveness.

If you are working on some solutions to social problems, you want others to participate. Just because other people are not similar to you, it does not mean that they cannot contribute. Include the recipients of the support when creating solutions for them. They truly understand the situation better.

With diverse people come diverse solutions, which need to be tested to get to the best solution. Poor people are not stupid; they just don't have a lot of money.

3) Appreciate others.

Expectations lead to disappointment. Trade your expectations for appreciation. If you are working towards a solution and the government or corporations do come to your support, acknowledge them for their contribution and be grateful. Don't expect the government or the charities to act a certain way, even if you think that it is their job.

Appreciate your co-founders, appreciate the volunteers. Do not take things for granted. People will find it enjoyable being around you.

Remember, being angry or feeling that the situation is unjust do not solve problems. Be in a state of mind that encourages you and others around you to try solutions, and not worry about the success or failures. Do it because you believe in the cause.

This is an empowering state of mind. You want to be in a state that encourages yourself and people around you to be innovative and come out with all sorts of fun solutions. The activity should be enjoyable and it should not feel like a "job".

11. Having More Social Enterprise is Not Enough

The very concept of a social enterprise is flawed. Every company pays taxes and hires people. They solve a certain need in society. Are they all considered social? What's more, when examining these concepts in practice, flaws are even further exposed.

I have been a judge at many startup competitions, and been invited to judge various social enterprises. On one hand, I am glad that more people are interested in social enterprises and are looking into sustainable ways to solve social problems, however, too many of them have ideas which are either businesses trying to look social, or charities trying to get more funds.

There is a supermarket chain in a country I've visited that is the the largest in the country. The company is a co-operative of the national trade union and is considered a social enterprise. Being one of the biggest supermarket chains, it also runs an insurance company and is involved in other for-profits businesses. There are also chains in other countries. Claiming to be a cooperative, this supermarket is declared as a social enterprise and became one of the largest social enterprises in the world, but I have yet to see any social mission of the company, which seems to be just a supermarket chain.

There are also various organizations supporting the handicapped by selling products made by the handicapped. However, in many cases, the products are not really produced by the handicapped people; they just added some details or help put it in a box. For a mug from these organizations to cost $25 with nothing special on it, people are buying it out of pity and not because they like or they need it.

Is a restaurant a social enterprise because it hires seniors at a lower wage to help clean the restaurant?

Is a hotel a social enterprise, because it hires some ex-convicts as staff?

Is a food truck a social enterprise because for every $10 hotdog you buy, they will donate some food to the food bank?

Sadly, many of these organizations consider themselves social enterprises, but operate just like normal businesses, sometimes taking advantage of marginalized people by hiring them but paying them a lower salary.

In my opinion, social entrepreneurs should not look at problems and try to sell products. When an entrepreneur sells something to people living in poverty, he may think he is a social entrepreneur, but there is a big difference between needs and wants. When you sell things to the poor that they don't need, it reduces their ability to save and get out of poverty.

The Flaws of Aid

TOMS Shoes is a social enterprise. If you buy a pair of shoes from them, they will give a pair of shoes to a child in the developing world with the understanding that proper footwear lowers parasite and infection rates. However, this idea is flawed. Hookworms and parasites are sanitation problems. Building latrines is the better and cheaper solution than free shoes. Further, these donated shoes hurt cobblers in those communities.

In Africa, donations of used clothes reduced garment sector employment by 50%, between 1981 and 2000. African poverty is a consequence of a general economic stagnation. Giving of any kind targets the symptom, not the disease. A more effective alternative would be to support local businesses by selling locally made shoes internationally, rather than bringing free ones into the community.

Aid often creates dependency. It does not create jobs or build capacity in a sustainable future.

Aid also gives governments less incentive to build effective institutions. Public revenue from taxes pegs the government to the success of their taxpayers. Free money, however, builds bloated bureaucracies. Rather than encourage businesses and job creation, it is easier to use someone else's money to create new government jobs.

Today, we have a lot of small scale social entrepreneurs trying to do good work through social projects. Some of these projects do have a lot of potential; however, there are a lot of considerations required before scaling can be done. The impact needs to be studied by an educational body (i.e., a university) to give the project more credibility, create more awareness, get corporate support and affect policy change. For those reasons, social innovation labs are increasingly common; working with such labs on social impact and studying success and failure of current projects is the way to move forward.

12. Case Study 1: Rescued Prostitutes

I've mentored many students on various projects. From polytechnics to universities, many of the students want to do something good, volunteer and help the needy. Their intentions are noble and their efforts are admirable.

In one of the projects, the students wanted to rescue prostitutes in Vietnam, start a factory and hire them. The idea was conceived when the students learnt about human trafficking and prostitution and wanted to take action.

The business plan looked pretty solid, financials were strong, and they researched on the different products they could sell. They even found mentors and connections in Vietnam, a location for the factory and calculated the costs for setting things up. The planning and work done was extensive and with the budget finalised, the students did fundraising and received donated sewing machines, allowing them to set up a factory in Vietnam.

With the connections made, 50 prostitutes were rescued from the brothels and given jobs in the newly setup factory. They were trained to make bag and pouches and the students created channels to sell these products.

The result was great; the women had a new way to make money to support their families and the training and operations went well, as with the sales. The students and several organizations they worked with called it a success and after six months, they won an award and went on with their lives.

A few months later, a new group of students was in the same program to set up social businesses in South East Asia, however, they did not choose to continue the same project, and started their own.

I happened to be in Vietnam for business and visited the factory as it was near one of my meeting locations. This was only slightly over a year since the project started but the factory seemed to be empty. There were only two people remaining in the factory and when I asked them if I was in the right place, they replied, "Yes, this is the factory. The others left because the Singer sewing machines broke down and we cannot find anyone to repair them locally. As more machines broke down, the ladies left as they still needed a job to support their families. Now there are two machines remaining."

I was shocked and asked, "So did they all…?" The two ladies nodded their heads. After a longer chat with the ladies over a meal, I learned more about their culture. In Vietnam, prostitution is socially acceptable as a means to support their family. The ladies were not as ashamed as people from other countries who view prostitutes differently, and they were not involved in human trafficking, but rather, had come to the city, were unable to find a job and needed money to support their families.

It was still a very nice effort of the students to make the business happen, but I just felt disappointed that their efforts were wasted as the project did not really last even for a year.

13. Case Study 2: Internet Comes to El Limón

Damian Durruty (ICT Specialist and Educator)

May 2014 marked the beginning of my third year of service as a Peace Corps volunteer in the Dominican Republic. Although the usual length of service is two years, I extended for a third year for practical reasons (pending projects) and out of sheer stubbornness (I refused to return to the U.S.). I wasn't a seasoned expert in the field of development, nor was I exactly a newbie.

Up until that point I had mostly been working with communities on the Haitian-Dominican border and had experienced varying degrees of success with the projects I helped execute in the region. Sometime during my second year, I met an American man named Jon whom I was later to befriend. He explained to me that he had been living in a village called El Limón for the past 15-20 years and working on all sorts of interesting projects. Eager to live somewhere different and work alongside a fellow American, I decided to relocate to El Limón at the start of my third year.

I was warned by Jon that El Limón would be a difficult community to work with because of its lack of community organization and cohesion. I was up for the challenge, but Jon's cautioning proved to be spot on. Out of the three communities I worked with throughout the course of my Peace Corps service, El Limón was by far the most difficult.

El Limón is a rural community of about 300 *campesinos*[10] nestled in the hills of the province of San Jose de Ocoa, bordering on the country's arid southern region. There were impressive projects that Jon had spearheaded during his time there, projects that had advanced El Limón's technological development by decades. Although the community was agrarian and underprivileged, it could boast of wireless internet, a hydroelectric plant, a community kitchen, a training center for electronics workshops, and a rudimentary computer lab. Yet despite all of this infrastructure, and despite Jon's groundbreaking work, El Limón remained a community of contradictions: technologically advanced yet socially dysfunctional.

---

[10] Rural farmers

The village was plagued by an abnormally high teen pregnancy rate, even by Dominican standards. Virtually every teenage girl wound up pregnant before turning 18. There were no prominent leadership or authority figures in the community nor were there any community-led organizations actively involved in local society. The presence of two *colmados*[11] with ample supplies of beer and rum fomented a culture of alcoholism while harder drugs such as crack and cocaine were starting to gain traction. Generations of marriages between distantly related family members as well as exorbitant overuse of third-world pesticides on local crops had lead to a slew of health problems and birth defects that few families had the resources to deal with. Even El Limón's relationship with its environment was unhealthy, having historically relied on the destruction of trees for charcoal production as one of its primary income sources.

As I thought carefully about how this situation came to be, I found out that decades before Jon's arrival, a now deceased Canadian priest named Luis Quinn had established a powerful organization with a hierarchical leadership structure based on the Catholic Church's organizational structure. His institution performed some notable work, and Luis Quinn is somewhat respected in the various communities of San Jose de Ocoa, but the charitable work was not conducted with sustainability in mind: it was executed via a top-down model that placed himself at the top. After his passing, that power structure collapsed and the grassroots leadership went down with it. Communities never learned to fend for their own, instead expecting external organizations led by high-ranking agents to dole out resources and rescue them from their plight.

This social phenomenon was exacerbated by the fact that the Dominican Republic has traditionally been a country run by *caudillos,* or strongmen. The focus was never on cultivating new leadership but on retaining power and establishing hegemony. The result is that power is not distributed in a meritocratic manner, but dynastically or through tightly-knit, class-based relationships.

Jon is a brilliant man whom I have tremendous respect for. But even Jon's ingenuity could not solve the slow societal crisis that was brewing in El Limón. In some ways, the community was actually worse off than it was two decades ago, when a semblance of community leadership still existed. Unfortunately, this lack of community support undermined his efforts and compromised his vision of helping to develop a communal society of self-sufficient, agrarian technologists.

---

[11] Local general store

From the very beginning I struggled to get projects moving. There was a computer lab with internet that was in disrepair and wasn't being maintained. I worked hard for months to restore everything, set up and train a supervisory committee, establish accountability — all to no avail. The will just wasn't there. Within a couple months of my departure everything fell apart. While I did my best to cultivate local leadership, one year of service wasn't going to counteract years of social neglect.

I gave sex education workshops and found out later that nearly all the young girls who participated ended up as teenage mothers. A one-week workshop wasn't going to put a dent into a culture that continuously and surreptitiously encouraged adolescent motherhood. If the right conditions had existed, if I could have partnered with the right locals, and my efforts might have made a lasting difference. Alas, the circumstances weren't right for the type of work I was trying to do. My efforts weren't perfect by any stretch of the imagination, but they should have produced at least a tiny positive impact instead of a counterproductive one.

Social change is often slow and spans multiple generations. A foreigner lacking knowledge of local traditions, customs and history isn't going to be the harbinger of community cohesion. It's a lesson for future development specialists: if the social infrastructure isn't there, physical infrastructure projects will likewise fail, especially infrastructure requiring continuous local management. This is an important consideration that is frequently ignored, especially by groups that adhere to the traditional charity model of development.

A few important questions to consider when deciding on a project are: Who will maintain the project? What happens when something inevitably breaks? Who will manage everything and make sure that project resources aren't abused? Is the project something that the community actually wants (as opposed to something that an NGO wants for a community)? Where will funding come from? Who will manage finances? Are they trustworthy? Does the community have a history of successful projects? Does the leadership serve and respect the community, or are they self-serving?

I have high hopes that the people of El Limón will summon the collective will to confront its dilemma one day. But that change will ultimately have to come from within — it will have to be the community itself that decides to be the driver of its own change. External contributors can certainly accelerate the process, but foreign actors should ultimately aim to be facilitators or partners, and should selectively invest resources into communities capable of leveraging those resources.

14. Case Study 3: The Flower Lady

A message I share with all my volunteers on the disaster relief projects is, "Never help, instead, focus on the task you set out to do." This is, however, easier said than done.

Ten days after the tsunami in Japan, in 2010, we walked past a 60-year-old lady cleaning her florist shop, removing buckets of mud, one at a time, with her mom sitting in the corner watching. She was strong and determined, fighting hard to get her business started again. For many days, we saw her working as we went to and fro on various tasks like bringing fuel to heat shelters and checking with hospitals and other shelters if there were any essential things needed.

One day, as we were walking by, the handle of the lady's bucket snapped and she dropped the bucket of mud on the floor. Even though my mind told me not to go help, when the team proceeded into the shop, my body betrayed me.

The team helped move the heavy shelves out and the remaining mud in the shop was easily pushed out. The whole process took several hours. Everyone including me was satisfied with our efforts in helping. The lady thanked us and cried. She was very grateful for our help.

By most accounts, this story would be a good story to tell about helping others in a disaster zone. It seemed like a happy ending, but unfortunately, life goes on and the story continues. We saw the lady cleaning up her shop, bringing pails of sea water to clean off the remaining stains for the next few days, and then she stopped coming.

About a month later, we found her in a shelter. She looked tired and sad. The fighting spark that was in her eyes when we first met her was lost. When we chatted with the people around her, they commented that she was crying every day at the shelter. Finally, I chatted with the lady, who was glad to see me. I asked her why she was sad and she told me about her sudden realization that she had just lost everything, her home, her business and how she probably would not get a loan to restart her business.

This was the unintended consequence of helping. She did not need our help in cleaning up her flower shop. She did not ask, yet we took that away from her. It may have taken her a month to clean the shop by herself, but we did it in one day. It may be inevitable that she would realize her loss, but it would be much better for her to be empowered to clean her shop by herself. By achieving success without help, she may have had the confidence to be able to do more.

15. The Unequal Distribution of Resources

Many societies have come to a point where people feel that the unequal distribution of resources is part of life. Some of my friends in Singapore buy into the prosperity gospel — a religious belief among some Christians that financial blessing is the will of God for them, and that faith, positive speech, and donations will increase one's material wealth. Others join mega churches and believe that they should earn more in order to give more.

In the U.S., my conservative Republican friends dislike paying taxes and make socialism a dirty word. They also believe that people are poor because they are lazy, and seek ways to reduce social spending.

Resources are materials found in the environment that humans use for food, fuel, clothing, and shelter. These include water, soil, minerals, vegetation, animals, air, and sunlight. People require resources to survive and thrive.

Due to the difference in the environment that results in different natural conditions, resources are distributed differently across the globe. Countries that do not have the resources they need can trade for them. Sometimes, conflicts happen when countries try to control resource-rich territories.

Within individual countries and societies, there is also unequal distribution of resources. Today, the income gap is widening. Many people consume fewer resources than they need for survival and well-being. As a result, there is much poverty in these countries. However, not everyone in these countries is poor; there are also a few people controlling all the resources, making them very rich.

This unequal distribution of resources, the legacy of imperialism, is the result of human rather than natural conditions. But this problem is not only found in third world countries, many countries do see a large income gap and the number of "working poor" in these countries is also on the rise. In fact, the world's 62 richest people hold as much wealth as the bottom 3.5 billion in 2016.[12]

---

[12] https://www.oxfam.org/en/pressroom/pressreleases/2016-01-18/62-people-own-same-half-world-reveals-oxfam-davos-report

We praise billionaires for their charitable donations and philanthropy. But where do they get their massive wealth from? Many of these billionaires are driven to make as much money as possible at any cost. After making money, they hoard their wealth and give a small portion to charity while putting the rest in a tax free financial vehicle.

Corporations are also hoarding trillions of dollars; some say they hold it for a "rainy day", while some corporations focus on "tax efficiency" which most of us call "tax avoidance". If they were to spend it, the economy would instantly grow, and we could see more jobs with better pay. Strangely, the stock market is also rewarding companies for hoarding money, namely, software and healthcare companies which hoard the most cash.

Perhaps this is a result of our dysfunctional society, a society where people suffer from curable diseases simply because they cannot afford medical care — because they are too poor. There is massive income inequality in the world and many that could not earn a sufficient living require aid in order to get by.

In many societies, people with materialistic wealth are looked up to as idols. No matter where he gets his wealth from, be it corruption or unfair business practices which kill of other smaller competition, he gets more respect for having more.

Many aspire to accumulate wealth and will find all means to get there, and only when they are rich do they participate in philanthropy. This is the kind of mindset that creates the income inequality, where people around die from poverty and the need is created for billionaire philanthropists to come to the rescue.

We need to address the distribution of resources at the root. We need to treat people in our society with empathy and consideration. It is definitely possible to do well while doing good. Through social innovation, marginalized communities can be freed from a life bound by servitude and dependency.

Poor people are not stupid. They have ideas and aspirations, but lack resources to solve even their most immediate problems. They do not need the help from the billionaire philanthropists; they do not need aid and donations. They need to be included in deciding their future, and to be connected to resources and empowered to solve their own problems.

What we need is for people to rethink their consumption habits. Supporting chain stores just because they sell cheaper products, but who may exploit their workers in the different levels of supply chains, may not the best way to save money.

We need business owners who treat their workers with respect and encouragement. We should not worship billionaires because it will encourage people to accumulate their wealth at any cost.

Everyone plays a role to empower their communities and enable the ones who are marginalized to do more. Charities are temporary solutions and the main problem we need to address is the unequal distribution of resources.

Billionaire philanthropists and large corporations do not hold the solution to the problems we face today, it is up to us to take actions and accountability to make things right.

16. Giving Done Wrong

Back in 2004, during the Asian Tsunami, I planned to go to Banda Aceh, and found a Christian group going there. So I ended up as part of a team delivering food aid to the survivors. Their intentions were good. There was definitely a great need for food when many homes were destroyed.

Upon arrival, I was greeted by a scene of surreal disaster. The magnitude of disaster was beyond what I had thought. The destructive force of nature was more than I could have imagined. I arrived at the shelters and distributed the canned food which the group had brought along.

I was shocked to see a can of luncheon meat, and later, more cans of hotdogs. Indonesia is a Muslim country, and many of the survivors are Muslims. When I pointed it out, the others in the group did not see it as a problem. I even heard a comment, "If they are hungry, they would have to eat what is given to them." Indeed, there was no choice now, however, back in Singapore, when the canned food drive was called and when the donors knew where the food was going to be delivered, there was a choice then.

I tried to inform the survivors about the food, however, the food I brought was not the first batch of food that had arrived, and many of the Muslim survivors had consumed pork from the previous deliveries of food. There was an immediate loss of trust. All the good will built up was lost.

When I returned to Singapore, I informed the organization about the situation and the pork given to Muslims, however, the reply was, "We cannot control what people donate, beggars can't be choosers." I was disappointed and felt that many things could be done to improve the situation, and that by having more care and communication, such a scenario would have never happened.

17. Free Destroys the Economy

I've seen many heartwarming projects that are providing free items to the poor. Soup kitchens in low income areas give free food to residents, doctors provide free medical services in rural areas, free vegetables and fruits are provided in areas struck by natural disasters.

Many of these good intentions do impact a lot of people and lives are affected. It is clear that social intervention affects lives. But are there ever negative consequences?

I was in Haiti after the 2010 earthquake and was talking to some people in the tent city. I realized that many of them were doctors, engineers and other skilled labor who had lost their jobs after the earthquake. A group of friends managed to fix the stairwell of a hospital and we managed to get the hospital running again, but I visited Haiti a year after and found that many of the skilled labor were still sitting in the shelters. By this time, there were even more foreign doctors providing free medical services, foreign contractors fixing roads and foreign aid giving free food. Those who had their jobs taken by free labor from volunteers were happy to get aid to survive, but were not optimistic about getting a job. Four years after the Haiti earthquake, more restaurants, farms and stores were put out of business, and foreign aid was still flowing in.

I met a friend and was visiting some food banks and soup kitchens to share ideas on bootstrap financing and entrepreneurship. Many of these soup kitchens were new and expanding and during the course of a year, but I realized that the cafes near the soup kitchens were all closing down. These soup kitchens did not require anything from the patrons, and people from all over were coming for a free meal.

As an entrepreneur, I realized that the cafes have to pay rent, buy supplies and pay wages, and with an increasing number of customers going for the soup kitchens' free food, they could not sustain anymore, which meant that their workers would lose their jobs as well.

Charity and caring for poor people is important, however, throwing money and giving free things to the poor does not bring them out of poverty. There are consequences when "free things" are introduced into a community, and sometimes these consequences are not as intended.

I've seen a food bank providing food for people who help prepare the food and clean the environment, clean the church and the surrounding block, and later clean up after they eat. This has greatly reduced the number of people coming for just free food, and I would think those receiving the food would feel more deserving and would feel that they were also contributing to their community.

I visited Haiti in 2015; five years after the Haiti Earthquake, unbuilt infrastructure and chaos left by the natural disaster can still be seen. After years of collaboration with the U.S., food and shelter are continuously provided and the situation seems only to be getting worse.

Under Bill Clinton, Haiti's leaders were pressured to reduce the country's longstanding tariffs on imported food (including rice) from 50% to about 3%. The U.S. then began dumping cheap, taxpayer-subsidized surplus rice on the Haitian market, ostensibly for humanitarian reasons, but actually so that it could dispose of an otherwise unsellable product.[13]

Haiti was once an agricultural land with plantation lands and crops for France, but the cheaper U.S. rice undercut and effectively destroyed Haitian rice farming. A country that was largely self-sufficient in this staple in the 1980s was importing 80% of its rice by 2012.

The "aid" provided made Haiti unable to feed itself, and the food crisis and food dependency forces Haiti to open itself to global forces. With farmers unable to sell their produce, many moved to the city and the overpopulation was one of the factors for the high death rates and diseases that followed after the earthquake.

Haiti imports as much as 50% of its food now, mostly from the U.S. Today, Haiti is the second-biggest importer of U.S. rice in the world.

The World Bank and the International Monetary Fund (IMF) give loans to many African countries if they privatize their economies and allow western nations free access to their raw materials and resources. Ghana for example is blessed with an abundance of resources and they used to have prosperous rice farming communities which, through farming subsidies, could feed the nation. When the loans were withheld until the government stopped giving the subsidies, Ghana started to import rice. And as the farm business slowly failed from the cheap

---

[13] http://csd.columbia.edu/2012/06/16/domestic-production-vs-imports-for-rice-in-haiti-a-delicate-balance-to-strike/

imports, the price of imports slowly increased and now, Ghana has to loan money to import rice to feed the nation.

When I visit an area after a disaster, I am glad that the locals are fed, but I get concerned when aid continues to pour in, together with subsidized food. This is because the local economy is one that needs to recover as well, and without the local economy getting restored, there will not be a sustainable recovery, and in the long run, the people will be worse off, due to the abundance of "aid".

18. Good Intentions Fail

In many countries, the government officials have extensive visions and plans for economic reforms. A lot of funding goes towards these programs but either through poor execution, corruption or other unforeseen situations, the reforms never have much of an impact, even though they were made with good intentions.

That is not to say that reform does not benefit anyone; most of these economic policies that focus on social security and job growth benefit the business owners, investors and other rich people. Controlling all the economic data, a lot of these governments also do not share their failures or even the collected economic data, making it hard to find out what went wrong.

Over the past decade, Mexico has channeled an increasing number of resources into subsidizing the creation of low-productivity, informal jobs. These social programs have hampered growth, fostered illegality, and provided erratic protection to workers, trapping many in poverty. Informality has boxed Mexico into a dilemma: provide benefits to informal workers at the expense of lower growth and reduced productivity, or leave millions of workers without benefits.

In most countries, the same calls for raising consumption taxes on higher-income households to simultaneously increase the rate of growth of GDP, reduce inequality, and improve benefits for workers happen, but the governments rarely carry out these policies because many of the friends and the supporters of these government officials are higher income people. Most officials also do not like challenging a system in place and would rather stay at status quo.

In developing countries, many big companies are invited to build factories and create employment for many people. This will also bring in investors who buy out a lot of properties, and as more people move into the cities, these investors will just make profits from rental and their properties, causing inflation, but economic policies will also favor these investors, and they pay little tax. Meanwhile, the bulk of the population in the city suffers depressed wages and overcrowded infrastructure, while the price of everything increases.

All of these countries are democratic countries, and the voters will vote in the leaders with policies that would further the income gap, even when they are in the lower income group themselves.

> **Poor Construction**
>
> In Singapore, the government mandates a Community Involvement Program (CIP) where students need to fulfil mandatory community service hours each year. The intention is for every student to develop a strong social conscience, and a sense of belonging and commitment to their community, society and country via experiential learning.
>
> I have heard about Singaporean students re-building an elementary school that collapsed in Nepal, as part of CIP. However, as the students did not have any experience in construction, and believed that construction was a low skilled job, they only did their research online, and a group actually went to Nepal to build a school.
>
> Although they sourced the materials locally, they decided to do all the work themselves. This included building walls of the school with bricks, and placing a zinc roof on top. However, with no experience in mixing cement, or even stacking bricks or layering the bricks, the school they built did not last more than a few months.
>
> I am sure these students had the best of intentions to build a more permanent structure for the children in that neighbourhood, but building a structurally unsound building without any supervision from a trained engineer, in an earthquake prone country that just suffered an earthquake just sounds foolish and dangerous.

Good intentions are often not enough. How many Fortune 500 companies from the 1950s are no longer with us today? I'm sure the executives in these companies had good intentions when they were making decisions which ultimately caused the company to fail, and most of these executives were professional and competent people.

Expansion Failure

The aggressive expansion of Krispy Kreme Doughnuts in the 1990s and 2000s both regionally and globally made the company go public in April 2000 and made the price of the share soar up to about $50 in 2003. However, in 2005, it posted a $198 million in losses and with an accounting scandal cause by a pressure to exceed projected earnings, the share prices tumbled 90% and many of the stores closed down. Fortunately for its fans, a few stores still remain in business.

Sticking-to-Original-Methods Failure

Some businesses stayed true to their methods and did not implement dramatic change. Borders and Blockbuster, both big businesses, limited their expansion plans to brick and mortar merchandizing strategies when their competitors went the online route. And the failure to evolve led to the closure of most of their stores and eventually the closing of the companies.

Innovation Failure

The executives at Coca-Cola attempted to improve on the tried and tested recipe for Coke, and abandoned the original recipe, introducing New Coke in 1985. New Coke was hated by purists and the media went to town with the story. Within three months, "Classic Coke" returned to the shelves after it had been retired.

Intuition Failure

Many people rely on their intuition — their gut feeling — to make decisions. But many do not realize that intuition fails constantly. Intuition may serve us well initially, but if we don't think deeper and use logic, we may be wrong.

> Example:
>
> A bat and ball cost $1.10.
>
> The bat costs one dollar more than the ball.
>
> How much does the ball cost?
>
> If you used your intuition, your answer would be $0.10.
>
> If you used logic, you would have answered $0.05.

Even top students from Harvard or MIT with perfect SAT scores would get it wrong. Many people are overconfident, prone to placing too much faith in their intuitions.

So even for some simple problems, you may need to put in more thought. They may not be as easy as you think.

Even big companies with the top executives and the best of intentions fail. And when businesses fail to deliver, they go out of business. When large NGOs or governments with the best of intentions fail to fix problems, chances are, they will ask for more funds to try again.

Good intentions are not enough. There is always the need for environmental change, technological change, and for methods we used in the past to aid those in need to evolve. We cannot plan to succeed with good intentions but without innovation. And what's worse, good intentions may yield bad consequences.

However, in some cases, the motive behind the actions may be far from altruistic.

Example: Sugar for EU (Cambodia)[14]

The initiative, Sugar for EU, was intended to fight poverty in developing countries, but has led to the sugar industry grabbing the land of 12,000 Cambodian small farmers and their families, leaving them destitute.

In 2008, no sugarcane was grown in Cambodia. Today, more than 100,000 hectares are dedicated to the crop. Forests and protected areas are being destroyed and thousands of smallholders and their families are being driven from their land by armed men.

The villagers often have no choice but to work as laborers on the plantations for which the land was stolen from them. Their homes and lands have been burnt to make way for the sugar plantations on which even the children have to work to make ends meet.

Many initiatives benefit the people n power, the people with connections; the poorest and most vulnerable people sometimes are worse off than before.

---

[14] https://www.rainforest-rescue.org/petitions/1012/cambodia-sugar-for-the-eu-is-destroying-our-landw

19. Case Study 4: Sanitation Woes

There are many infographics that show you that billions of people do not have access to proper sanitation. Sanitation is a concept that encompasses water supply, safe disposal of human waste, waste water and solid waste, domestic and personal hygiene. It is one of the basic determinants for quality of life.

Jack Sim runs the World Toilet Organization and I've seen him do great work providing lots of toilets to rural areas. He often talked about how he changed the mindsets of the people to view toilets as something desirable to own, and the local people actually bought and installed toilets in their homes. Sanitation is very important as poor sanitation leads to a whole slew of health issues and diseases.

The World Toilet Organization is very successful in making sanitation accessible. They partner big corporations and redesign toilets, making them cheaper and suited local needs.

In countries with large populations like China and India, littering is common, and in the rural areas, open defecation can easily be found as well. I would say that campaigns that raise funds to build toilets are rather successful as I've seen more toilets in my travels now than before, however, I still feel that the attitudes towards open defecation have not changed.

Toilets are subsidized and built in many homes and public areas, yet you can see parents encouraging their children to "go" in the open. And sometimes, even when the toilets are within walking distance, people still decide to openly defecate.

However, in other areas and in parts of Africa, I've seen villages with no toilets, yet the villagers will dig holes in specific areas to defecate and clean up and bury their waste. Sometimes I wonder if access to toilets should be the primary concern if people are not educated on the basic importance of sanitation first.

20. Case Study 5: They Ate the Chickens

I met up with friend who has an egg farm and after visiting Haiti for disaster relief, I returned to start a social business. In a small village, I met up with a few families and found that they were doing little economic activities which gave them a daily wage of about $7. One of them was involved in buying a big bag of rice, carrying it up the village 15 miles away, and selling cups of rice, making very little money. As I saw that most of their food and things they use are imported, I felt that eggs would be a cheap source of protein which people could use.

In the village that I engaged with, they were already doing basic farming and could feed the chickens grown or found on their farm. I provided $2,000 of funding to buy wires, and trained them to make chicken coops with wires and wood. I also bought hens and trained the villagers to feed the hens with what they grew in the village.

The villagers collected empty egg cartons, cleaned the eggs and sold them at the market. I bought a few roosters and taught the villagers how to fertilize the eggs. When everything is set up from the breeding of chicks to the selling of eggs, the daily income could go as high as $50.

When I was confident that they could run the farm on their own, I informed them that they could own this business and all I wanted was for them to pay me what I had spent on the farm. Within three months, they managed to pay me the $2,000 I put in and I was able to replicate the same project in Kenya, Brazil and Indonesia.

After four farms, I decided that if this initiative was so successful, I should write about it and get more communities to set up egg farms. So while I was doing my research and preparing for a TED talk, I started calling the villages I was working with more than a year ago. As I started to gather information, I was shocked to find out that the chicken farm in Haiti no longer existed. The villagers had eaten the chickens.

When I started to call the other farms, including Indonesia — the last farm I had visited only nine months ago, I realized that all of the egg businesses no longer existed. They had eaten all the chickens.

They could make more than six times their salaries with the egg farms, and yet, had decided to eat all the chickens. It was not a cultural factor either as the farms were located on different continents. This was when I realized one thing — is helping really having any sustainable social impact?

In many of these countries, I was there only for a short period of about one month each visit. I was looking at the project from my perspective and experience and not from the community's. Life in these villages is much more challenging than life in the city. They have no power and are constantly facing natural disasters and bad weather.

Everyone will accept a job when you promise them a 10-time pay raise. But as long as they see it as a job or an external project and not take ownership, they will always be the "employee" in a restaurant — when you order anything with eggs and they run out of eggs, they will tell you it is sold out, rather than be like the owner who will run down to the grocery store to get eggs to fulfil the order.

21. Case Study 6: Community Involvement Program Gone Wrong

In Singapore, students are required to participate in a program called (Community Involvement Program) CIP. the purpose is to nurture students to become more socially responsible. But has it genuinely yielded the relevant benefits?

The motivation of a compulsory program like this is not from altruism, but rather seen as a "no choice" situation. Also, volunteerism is low on the priority list for many of the working professionals who have gone through CIP previously.

I run Relief 2.0 and when I was working on a social business workshop in Fukuoka, Southern Japan was hit by heavy rain. Parts of Kyushu were flooded and the damage was quite extensive. I decided to see if anyone was interested in coming to Kyushu to help with the clean up after the floods and a few student groups responded.

I was introduced to CIP for the first time and after interviewing a few students and choosing six of them, I informed them about the dangers, what to expect and the things they have to do, and they agreed. A checklist was provided for them on what to wear and what equipment to bring and they were off to Japan.

Relief 2.0 would be responsible for their lodgings and some basic costs to cover some of their expense and food for 10 days, and the students would have to pay for their plane tickets and other travel expenses if they chose to travel after their disaster relief duties.

I planned for the students to work with Foreign Volunteers Japan who have a group cleaning up after the floods This group had transport and worked with the locals on helping the elderly home owners clean and dry the wooden floors of their flooded houses. I also found housing near Kyushu University in Fukuoka.

I gathered from the interviews that all the students selected seemed very passionate to learn and understand the dynamics of disaster relief. When they arrived, all of the girls wore heels and had not brought boots because they did not own any. As I was busy planning for the social business workshop, I got a few Japanese students from Fukuoka University to help them with shopping for equipment needed to do disaster relief work. The students then planned their route to meetup with Foreign Volunteers Japan. It involved getting on the 5:50am train and connecting with a bus to meet Foreign Volunteers Japan at 7:30am where the van would pick them up to work at the disaster area.

After they shared their plans with me, I double checked the route and it seemed reasonable. I requested that they start a journal to document their journey.

I received a phone call on Day 4 from Foreign Volunteers Japan. They asked me if the students were coming at all. I was confused and I went to meet up with the students to ask and it was only then that I realized that they had not been to the disaster site at all. The students woke up late and missed the train, took the next train but missed the connecting bus, and so returned. On the second day, the girls felt the boots were uncomfortable and went back to the mall to change for a bigger size and did not go to the disaster area again, and they bought alcohol and were drunk and did not go the following day either.

I was confused. These students who were so enthusiastic when I interviewed them seemed to show so much passion, but when they arrived, they seemed to be unprepared and unmotivated. I made it a point to wake them up at 5am to make sure they get to the 5:50am train and on Day 5, they finally went to the disaster area.

At this point, I was quite disappointed that I had picked these students, so I decided to ask them about their experience after the 10 days were over. They all wrote fantastic reports on the tiring but rewarding experience they had and how much they learnt helping the elderly clean their houses.

I shared this experience with some of my friends running NGOs in Singapore and they informed me that it was glamorous to go to an overseas CIP, and that experiences like mine were common but that they sometimes do get exceptional students who perform beyond expectation.

22. Social Technology

Technology changes the way we behave. In a short span of 30 years, we have we have transited from the telephone to the mobile phone to the smart phone. Not only does the way we communicate change, how we do things, our cultures and behaviors shift with technology too.

A lot of modern technology is also getting affordable. With the shrinking in sizes of computers, the smart phone today is more powerful than computers 20 years ago and the cost is coming down such that even people living in slums, villages and other poorer communities own these computers in their pockets.

Frugal innovation or frugal engineering is the process of reducing the complexity and cost of a good and its production. Usually this refers to removing nonessential features from a durable good, such as a car or phone, in order to sell it in developing countries.

This makes a lot of technology available to the masses, and has proven to be both a boon and a bane.

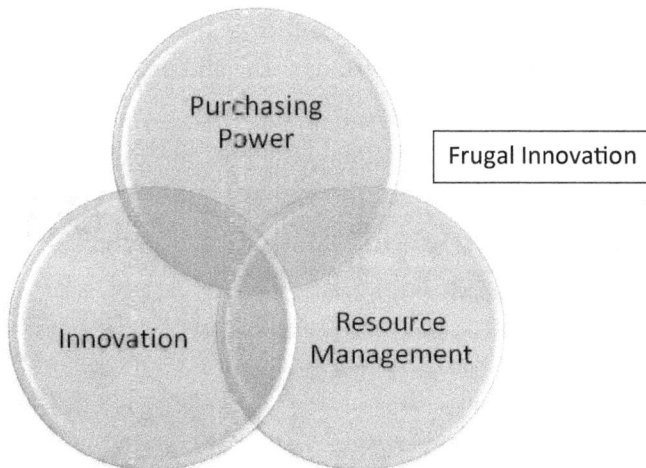

Purchasing Power

Frugal Innovation

Innovation

Resource Management

With affordable smart phones, the internet is now accessible to millions, and mobile transactions can save a lot of time and paper. They also have access to a lot of information online, and the cost of communications can also be much reduced.

On the other hand, affordable cars do create a whole lot more pollution when the masses can now afford to drive.

Persuasive Technology

Today, technology can be designed to change attitudes or behaviors of the users through persuasion and social influence, but not through coercion.

We have already experienced this in many ways. The installation wizard when you install a software helps people with limited knowledge of computers and software complete their tasks easier. Technologies that convert speech to text and translate are getting common for online streaming videos to allow us to watch foreign movies in languages we do not understand.

War

War is a terrible thing. When nations, states or different groups of people within a state engage in armed conflict, everyone suffers. Since World War 2, the economically strongest nations have enjoyed the longest period without fighting each other.

The causes of war include statism, conflict of ideology or control over trade routes or resources. War also causes serious social and psychological damage to the society which is hard to recover from.

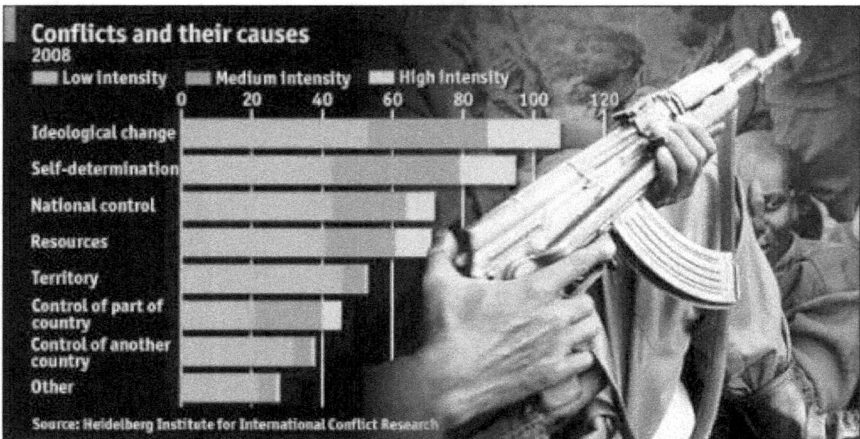

Conflicts and their causes
2008
Low intensity   Medium intensity   High intensity

Source: Heidelberg Institute for International Conflict Research

Many of the humanitarian crises occur due to war where homes are destroyed and people are forced to leave their homes. There will also be humanitarian, economic, development and security issues created which require a lot of resources to fix.

It may be very hard to stop a war and the consequences are grave, and it may just be smarter to prevent a war.

Peace

Peace is not the opposite of war, it encompasses a lot more. It includes harmonious coexistence of different groups of people living together, sharing the environment, co-creating and collaborating together.

23. Peace Technology, Social Innovation and Entrepreneurship

Is it possible to create positive peace?

With existing technology, research and studies, in the fields of behavior design, innovation, social technology and finance, it is possible to prototype and create sustainable positive peace. Creating multiple ways to allow everyone on both sides of a possible conflict to engage allows them to learn more about each other.

Perhaps one of the main causes of peace is capitalism: the social system based on the principle of individual rights, the idea that each individual has a moral prerogative to live his life as he sees fit (the right to life); to act on his own judgment, free from coercion by others (liberty); to keep and use the product of his effort (property); and to pursue the goals and values of his choice (pursuit of happiness).

When people create economic activities, trade and support themselves, it reduces the chance for a conflict. In every bordertown that has strong economic activity, there are far more collaborations and people on the bordertowns who speak both languages and know more about each other's religion. When people cross the border to work or to set up factories, economic development will also reduce the desire of the governments to have a conflict.

Stanford has a peace innovation lab, an initiative from persuasive technology lab. It focuses on real world interventions to reduce conflict and precursors to conflict, through exploration on rapid innovation, behavior design, persuasive technology, trust, design for empathy, and game design thinking among others.

Companies can also utilize on these persuasive technologies to bring positive changes in their domains, including health, business, safety, and education. Technology can be designed to influence human beliefs and behaviors.

Social Innovation

Social innovations are new strategies, concepts, ideas and organizations that meet the social needs of different elements which can be from working conditions and education to community development and health — they extend and strengthen civil society. Social innovation includes the social processes of innovation, such as open source methods and techniques and also the innovations which have a social purpose — like online volunteering, microcredit, or distance learning.

The Need for Social Innovation

There are many social problems. Most are more complex than they seem and when solutions come from one discipline or are simply focused on "patching" the problem, the problem rarely gets solved and often becomes more complex as time goes by.

> "Philanthropy dollar" can only be used once, the "social dollar" can be used again and again.
>
> — Muhammad Yunus

Social Enterprise

Social enterprise is a form of Social Innovation. A social enterprise is an organization that applies commercial strategies to maximize improvements in human and environmental well-being — this may include maximizing social impact rather than profits for external shareholders.

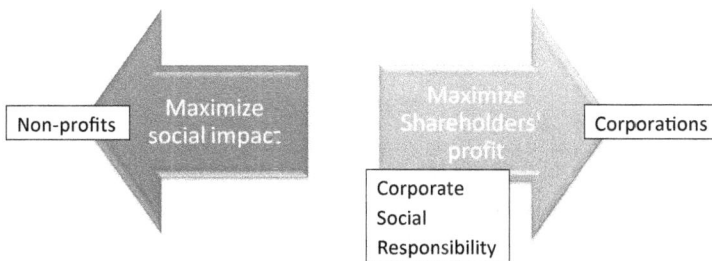

Social enterprise, like non-profits and charities, have important roles in society. Non-profit organizations play an important role of providing public services to communities where they operate, making them an intermediary between citizens and authorities.

Non-profits perform a variety of tasks and they largely get their funding from donations and grants. They are allowed to make profits, and they will not be taxed as long as profits generated will be used to achieve the mission. They also operate no under distribution constraints and are responsive to donors and board members.

A social enterprise is a business that adopts a social value and exhibits a heightened sense of accountability towards the constituents served. As a business, it has to make a profit to be sustainable, and the profits can go towards individuals running the organization.

Corporations are businesses that focus on maximizing shareholder value. Their primary goal is to make a profit for the owner.

Governments get their funding from taxes and are accountable to the voters. There is a lot of bureaucracy in the way of getting things done and the projects are generally large scale.

Mission Driven

Money Driven

Government
Non-profit

Corporations

Government	Non-profit	Corporations
Large scale solutions	Mission driven	Primarily focused on profits
Focus on equity	Operate under non-distribution constraints	Market sensitive
Slow moving and cautious	Creative and adaptive to local conditions	Fast to respond
	Often shaped by values and faith	Competition driven
Accountable to voters	Responsive to board, community, donors and public	Responsive to shareholders

There are a lot of gaps in society, and when there is no obvious profit, corporations and businesses tend to not fill the needs as they have be responsible to shareholders.

The government is slow to act and tends to do large scale projects as they are cautious and unable to react to fast changing conditions as bureaucratic approvals are required for most spending.

Non-profits are often focused specifically on missions aligned to them. They also have many constraints as funding comes from donors. When there is a recession and people's needs increase, the funding generally decreases as well.

There are two great forces of human nature: self-interest and caring for others. Capitalism harnesses self-interest in helpful sustainable ways, but only on behalf of those who can pay. Philanthropy and government aid channel our caring for those who can't pay, but the resources run out before they meet the need to provide for the poor. We need a system that draws in innovators and businesses in a far better way.

With the increased frequency of natural and man-made disasters, we need new ways to solve old problems. There is a need for changemakers to take risk and drive innovation, not just because it may be profitable, but also because it is the right thing to do.

These changemakers can also collaborate with the government, non-profits and corporations to get things done. They are known as social entrepreneurs.

Social Entrepreneurship

I have 4 criteria for social entrepreneurship:

1) Innovation

2) Financial sustainability

3) Impact

4) Scale

The project needs to be able to make a profit on its own without exploiting the environment and should be able to collaborate with other organizations to maximize impact.

The goal for social entrepreneurship is to create innovative, sustainable, effective and scalable solutions to social problems.

Social entrepreneurship can solve many problems and with a good financial model, can be sustainable. Together with other initiatives, many communities will benefit. However, there are many other progressive models out there that would change the social landscape.

Larger corporations are engaging in Corporate Social Responsibility, and when done well, they can do a lot of social impact as they are very well funded and have a lot of resources to tap on. Charities are also evolving and many of them are trying to find ways to get income to subsidize their lack of donations.

24. CSR 2.0

Corporate social responsibility (CSR, also called corporate conscience, corporate citizenship or responsible business) is a form of corporate self-regulation integrated into a business model.

Many companies have started their CSR programs, and some of them have linked a small percentage of their profits to giving, while others run annual fundraising for charities. Some of the law firms give pro-bono work while some companies give time off for employees to volunteer.

But traditional corporate social responsibility is failing to deliver, for both companies and society. In most cases, the companies attempt to be seen as more social because of some public backlash of the scandals which they were caught doing, and others simply are using this as a pure marketing ploy, with a two-man CSR team in a 500-man company.

Even for the genuine cases where these companies want to have real social impact, what went wrong, and why does traditional CSR fail to deliver?

Firstly, the individual case of the CSR failure of each company differs, and we can break them up into three simple questions:

How are the companies doing on external engagement?

Where have they gone wrong?

What can be done better?

How are the Companies Doing on External Engagement?

When it comes to the first question, already many of the companies which I've researched on fail. External engagement does not just mean corporate philanthropy, it should involve a lot of other programs that include community engagement, product design, project execution, recruiting policy.

Many companies have a one- or two-men CSR team, very little resources, and they simply have little budget for a corporate philanthropy dinner, pledging some profits to a charity. For most cases, even the employees themselves do not know about the CSR efforts, let alone the outside world.

While some companies seem to have a little bit of impact on the community, most CSR initiatives are unknown and executives recognize that their current approach is inadequate.

During the occupy movements, the corporations are shown as the villains. Even the companies with big CSR budgets are not spared. In most countries, there is little trust in most corporations, and some people have the view that corporations are enriching themselves at the expense of the communities.

With the bail outs of the banks after the financial crisis, bail out of the airlines, BP oil spills in the Gulf of Mexico and numerous other cases of unfair government lobby to pay less taxes, public trust is at an all-time low.

The expectations of consumers and the public have also been higher, and with the food scandals and GMO crops, businesses need to ensure a higher standard not only in their own business, but along their supply chains.

Large companies now are expected to solve economic, environmental and social problems, and every little flaw that they commit is scrutinized. With digital media, citizens can observe and monitor all sorts of activities of a company and launch petitions and campaigns when they get offended by some perceived unfair practices. Crisis often happens and successful companies must be prepared to deal with them in a transparent and fair way. Otherwise, they can expect severe repercussion in the drop of their share prices and lose billions of dollars as a result.

Where have they Gone Wrong?

In large companies, even a well-supported CSR team backed by the CEO may fail to deliver on their core purpose. And one of the main reasons is that this CSR team is separate from the rest of the company and exists just as a department.

Head office will give this team a budget and not really communicate with it much, and decide to slash the budget when profits are down. This translates to an abrupt end to many programs due to lack of funding (when times are bad, these programs may need more funding) and budget cuts. Without active participation, the finance department can decide on the budget without considering the needs of the CSR team and marketing and operations of the CSR team may be severely impacted.

Additionally, the CSR team without interaction with the rest of the company may lose touch with reality and have a different perspective on what is going on in the company. For some part-time CSR teams, they may not have enough time for external engagement and may not understand the problem in its context, thus having difficulties in solving it.

In some companies which are starting out CSR projects, they tend to have a short time frame for success. These companies would like to do short term projects and expect big impact. The executives providing the funds expects constant reporting and measurable impact even when they do not provide enough resources for the project.

Lastly, many corporations want to do CSR, but only projects related to their industry or to protect their reputation especially after a crisis.

So What can be Done Better?

CSR can be more than just donations and volunteering. It can attract new customers, motivate and retain employees, and win over governments. A fact that is often forgotten is that all companies operate in a community. And community engagement is very important part of business. Whenever the business makes a decision which may affect the community, public consultation should be done and external considerations need to be part of the business making process.

The external world and the immediate community are full of potential customers and staff, regulators, activists and legislators. People who can share their experience of their engagement with the business on the digital media and others in their networks can know.

Many large companies have a big marketing team and social media reach. Many smaller NGOs that are doing good social impact often do not have much of a capacity to spread awareness of their cause. A good solution is simply to allow some employees in the marketing team to work on infographics and messages to support local NGOs. These are some skills the marketing team already possesses, and sharing it on the company's social media would also promote the virtues of the company. The employees can also feel that they are doing something meaningful and may increase staff retention.

CSR should not be just donations for sustainability. CSR leadership development creates a cool company to work, and improves employee retention. In many forward thinking organizations, CSR is so in line with business that the word social does not even need to be uttered and business practices will consider many social and environmental aspects before implementing.

Many companies may preach their values to their customers but how many of them talk about their virtues?

CSR can also be co-created by NGOs and corporations and this collaborative engagement is key. Much empathy is needed and it can create a win-win situation for both parties. However, the corporate skills and NGO needs must match. It should not be done at the convenience of the corporation, but rather, done together as equals.

So whether the business think social media or CSR, this convergence should be part of the organization's DNA for the organization to be future ready and ready to withstand any social media crisis.

With engagement, a business can build trust, and change perception. The business can influence their customers to do the right thing and not just buy their product.

In my opinion, CSR converges with communications. A business needs to be good in communicating its virtues. There are a few simple steps to make it clear.

1) Define what you contribute.

Every company makes a significant contribution to society. Businesses offer goods and services people want. In the process, they provide capital, jobs, skills, ideas, and taxes. But many companies don't emphasize that contribution. Most companies can share their small CSR-related contributions to the public, where internally, they focus on what they get from society. But if a company exists only to make a profit from society and do one or two small donations to an NGO as part of their CSR, it undermines credibility.

Companies need to have a sustainable relationship with the external world. Instead of merely promoting their small CSR project, the companies should just define themselves through what they contribute. A good resolution is for an energy company to invest in clean energy, reducing their running costs and environmental impact.

A company should not just do CSR just to improve its image, it needs to have its virtues at the core of the company; virtues employees can relate to and share. This approach does not mean changing purpose; it means being explicit about how fulfilling that purpose benefits society. Nor does it mean abandoning a focus on shareholder value; it means recognizing that you generate long-term value for shareholders only by delivering value to society as well.

2) Engage with your stakeholders.

The stakeholders in the perspective of many companies are Customers and Shareholders. It is essential to be customer oriented, listening to customer feedback, understanding your consumer. With social media, it is easy for businesses to engage with customers and to promote their products. However, the engagement needs to be authentic. There is no high cost to social media, but it does require resources.

Today, with social media, stakeholders mean much more than just customers and shareholders. Employees and even people from the local communities should be considered stakeholders. Instead of fearing engagement and ignoring social media, new bold ways of transparent communications are key. It is important to build trust and have guidelines of engagement. Everyone in the company is a potential marketing person and everyone affects the corporate image. It is important for the virtues of the business to show through the employees, and have direct communication with the local communities to learn more about their needs, and find ways to contribute and know them better.

Business today is more of an experience than just a transaction. Running a business also cannot be done in a void and the local community and their needs need to be considered.

3) Empower your staff.

Employees all have different needs, hopes and aspirations. Attracting the right employee is very important and people need to be treated fairly. Employees are the core of the company and everyone has a critical role to play in the company. It is important for employees to be fairly compensated and to allow them time to contribute to the local community.

Employees should be allowed and empowered with a little autonomy to discover better ways of doing things instead of just following standard procedures. The next newest disruptive innovation is just around the corner, and sometimes, businesses have to embrace a culture of change and curiosity through its employees and adapt, or become obsolete.

If an employee discovers a better way of doing something, reward the employee. If the employee fails at a task, treat it as a learning example so others can know not to try it in the same way.

25. Social Intrapreneur

Intrapreneurship is known as the practice of a corporate management style that integrates risk-taking and innovation approaches, as well as the reward and motivational techniques that are more traditionally thought of as being the province of entrepreneurship.

In many large companies, there are employees who take responsibility for turning an idea into a profitable finished product through assertive risk-taking and innovation. Many of these employees are beneficial for their corporations. The relationship is also very beneficial. These employees innovate for the company, and the company funds them and provides corporate resources.

With many large companies embracing Intrapreneurship, there is also a growing trend of Social Intrapreneurship. Today, as more companies embrace CSR, Social Intrapreneurs are making traditional CSR models look irrelevant. By adapting entrepreneurial strategies, employees of public and non-profit sectors can improve the organizations with hybrid value models, cost saving innovations and enhanced efficiencies.

Social Intrapreneurship is a relatively new thing. In 2014, BMW Foundation, CSR Europe, and Asoka announced their 2014 Social Intrapreneurship Europe Program. Social Intrapreneurs can be found in all levels of the company innovating for social good. However, many of them still struggle against the bureaucracy of their organizations. There are still many challenges ahead for these Social Intrapreneurs as they may not get enough support or resources from their organizations in order to scale their impact.

In time, with more awareness created as social intrapreneurship gains more momentum, social intrapreneurs may soon be the most valuable employees at many companies as they are good for the bottom line, good for the brand and good for staff morale. And the solutions they bring along could solve the world's most pressing problems.

More information on Social Intrepreneurship can be found at:

https://www.techchange.org/2013/09/30/what-is-intrapreneurship/

https://www.youtube.com/watch?v=5KYWJdU9Ltw&feature=youtu.be

26. Social Business

"Poverty is a threat to peace."

— Muhammad Yunus

The Social Business Concept

Unlike traditional business, a social business operates for the benefit of addressing social needs that enable societies to function more efficiently. Social business provides a necessary framework for tackling social issues by combining business know-how with the desire to improve quality of life. Professor Yunus, winner of the Nobel Peace Prize 2006, has already demonstrated the effectiveness of this new type of business: his clear focus on eradicating extreme poverty combined with his condition of economic sustainability has created numerous models with incredible growth potential. The framework of a social business is based on seven principles. With the idea of social business, Prof. Yunus has introduced a new dimension for capitalism: a business model that does not strive to maximize profits but rather to serve humanity's most pressing needs.

Non-loss, Non-dividend Company solving a social problem.

	NGO / Public Sector	Social Business	Traditional Business
Ends	Social / Ecological use Maximization	Social / Ecological use Maximization	Profit Maximization
Means	Donation Financed	Self- Sustainable	Self- Sustainable

"Social business unites the dynamism of traditional business with the social conscience of charity."

— Muhammad Yunus

Six Principles of Grameen Social Business

1. Business objective will be to overcome poverty, or one or more problems (such as, education, health, technology access, environment, etc) which threaten people and society; not profit maximization.

2. Financial and economic sustainability.

3. Investors get back the investment amount only. No dividend is given beyond investment money.

4. When investment amount is paid back, company profit stays within the company for expansion and improvement.

5. Environmentally conscious

6. Workforce get market wage with better working condition.

7. do it with Joy

Seven Principles: The Principles of Social Business

1. Business objective will be to overcome poverty, or one or more problems (such as education, health, technology access, and environment) which threaten people and society; not profit maximization

2. Financial and economic sustainability

3. Investors get back their investment amount only. No dividend is given beyond investment money

4. When investment amount is paid back, company profit stays with the company for expansion and improvement

5. Environmentally conscious

6. Workforce gets market wage with better working conditions

7. Do it with joy

27. Design Thinking and Social Innovation

Social problems are extremely complex and many of them are affiliated with a lot of "baggage" about how they ought to be solved. Many of them have been around for years and the conventional problem solving methods have not worked so far. Design thinking allows us to shed much of that baggage, leading to an innovation.

Social problems are entrenched and require new, innovative methods to solve them in financially sustainable ways. It requires innovation not just in the product or service but also often in the delivery, financial model, partnerships, etc.

When there is a problem, non-profits may fill the needs by providing aid. As long as the non-profit can get funding and continue to provide aid, it does not need to innovate or solve the problem. There is also no reason to motivate the non-profit to change, because testing and prototyping may lead to failure which may have negative social impact.

Many creative people and companies use design thinking. Design thinking is a formal method for practical, creative resolution of problems and creation of solutions, with the intent of an improved future result. In this regard it is a form of solution-based, or solution-focused thinking — starting with a goal instead of solving a specific problem.

The Design Process

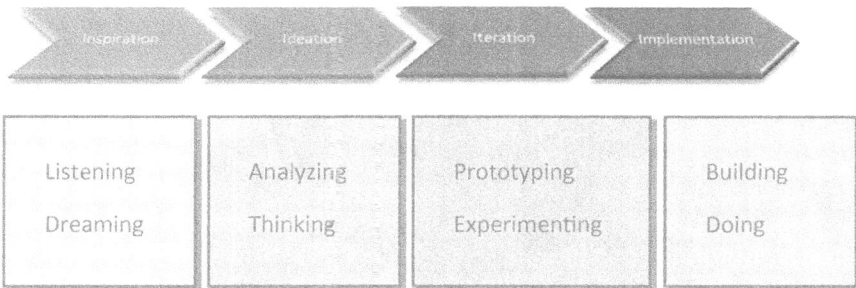

Inspiration	Ideation	Iteration	Implementation
Listening	Analyzing	Prototyping	Building
Dreaming	Thinking	Experimenting	Doing

Inspiration

Inspiration starts with listening. Listening is a process where the goal is not just to find the answers, but also to ask the right questions. Challenge your assumptions by suspending your beliefs.

Ideation

Organize and synthesize ideas

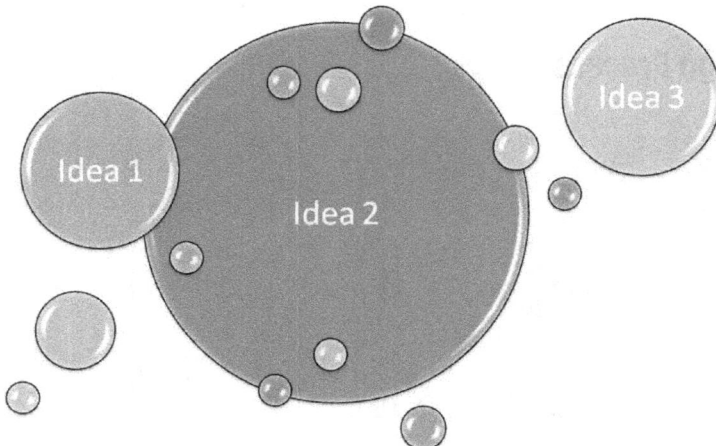

The goal is to identify patterns and relationships.

- Extract key insights
- Sort ideas (by level of magnitude)
- Find themes
- Create frameworks

Look at the 10 most important insights from the inspiration process and sort them by their magnitude. Look for similarities and themes and group them together.

Frameworks

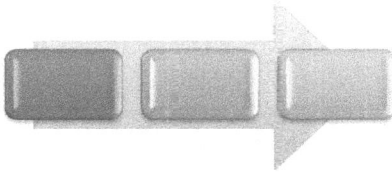

Process Map

Venn Diagrams

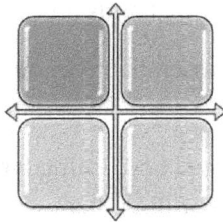

2x2 Matrix

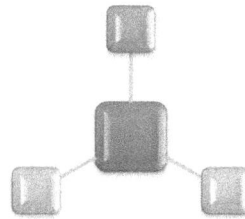

Mind Map

Mind map

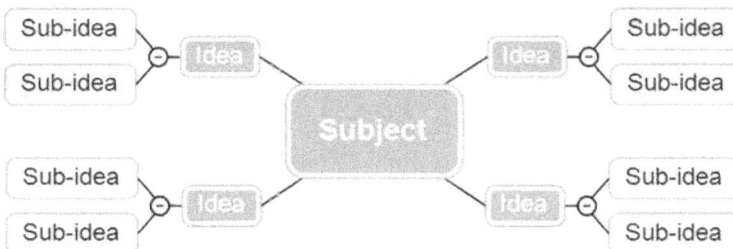

Iteration

Iteration begins with prototyping. In prototyping, it is important to know that perfection is not needed.

Prototyping begins with identifying the different models you can build.

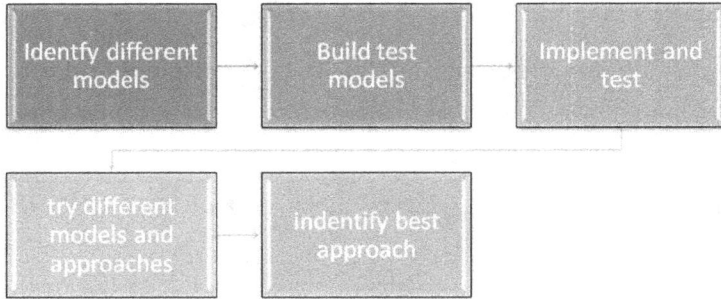

Where does innovation come from?

1) Challenging and abandoning previous assumptions

2) Uncover hidden truths

3) Discovering opportunities for improvement by hands on experience

4) Vigorous disassembly and methodically reassembly to understand and incorporate new discovery

5) Iterative process of taking nothing for granted and testing far flung ideas to proof that they do not work rather than discarding them without testing

6) Obsessive pursuit of new ways by taking nothing for granted and owning up to failures and learning from them

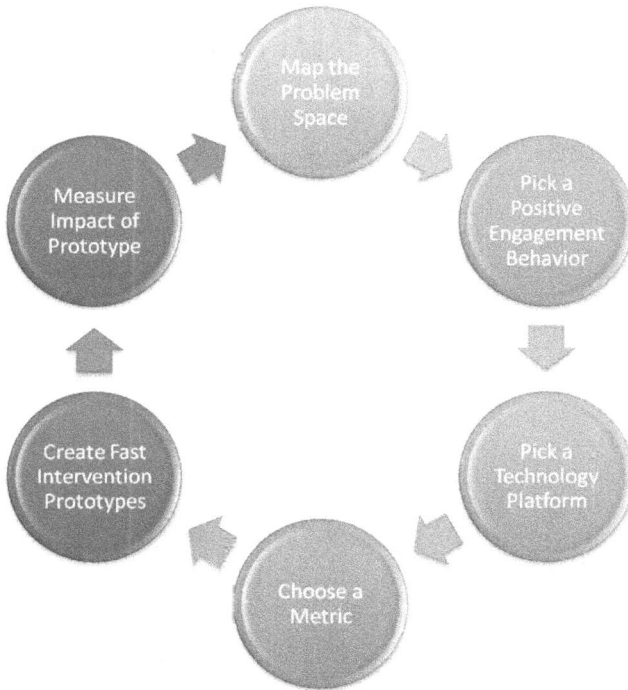

Rapid Social Intervention

Social Innovation focuses on new work and new forms of business models, especially those that work towards a sustainable society.

In many cases, rapid social interventions can start to bring positive change to communities, and putting a sustainable plan around the interventions can make it sustainable. It may eventually become a social enterprise.

28. Social Community

The Power of Crowds

Communities have the ability to solve their problems.

— They understand the problems they face better than anyone else.

— They are not stupid and can solve many problems.

— They don't need pity, donations or continuous aid.

— They must be allowed to try new ideas to get out of their bad situation and allowed to fail and learn from the experience.

Billions go into fighting poverty and yet more people fall into poverty everyday. NGOs have provided food, medicine and shelter for people, but require more and more funding as it does not address the problem. Giving food to people today does not reduce their need for food tomorrow.

Social Enterprise and social business ideas have a lot of potential, but I've encountered many great businesses which seem to be doing well and expanding fast but which cease to exist within two years of expansion.

Success — Scale — Fail

Running a small scale business to benefit a small group of people may prove to be successful, but when these social enterprises scale, most of them tend to fail.

Social Enterprises tend to run on a lean model, with limited budget to hire top talent. Most of the time, this is enough to have a profit and the founders do not ask for much, and believe in spending less and doing more, however, like most charities, this does not attract the talent and experience needed for it to scale.

Many Social Enterprises like startups are nimble and adaptive, but as the organization gets bigger, bureaucracy sets in and it is harder to deal with the changes on the ground. Some Social Enterprises get funding from VCs who seem to focus on returns, and the focus of social impact may become send to the focus on generating profits.

There is a great need for social innovation. Most issues are more complex than they seem and when solutions come from only one discipline or are simply focused on "patching" the problem, the problem rarely gets solved and often becomes more complex as time goes by.

Why Communities?

Marginalized communities are not helpless communities. There is untapped human capacity. Communities are capable to solve their own problems in the long run. People in similar communities can benefit from their solutions.

There are many other benefits from an engaged community. It is a mindset change and training marginalized communities to view problems as opportunities is important.

These communities know their problems and environment best, what they lack may be resources and options. When they think of solutions, they may not have a broad perspective due to the lack of external experience, however, the internet is readily available to change their perspective and provide knowledge and options.

When local solutions are found, scaling to other areas can be done to benefit many others.

Resources that they are receiving can be directed at other problems once communities can be independent and are able to solve their own problems. A pay-it-forward model can be created where the community supported can go and support other communities.

Helping marginalized communities is continuous. Donations to marginalized communities have one life; once used, more donations are needed. Empowering communities to support themselves will be a sustainable way to bring more options to the community.

"Social entrepreneurs are…the practical dreamers who have the talent and the skill and the vision to solve problems [and] to change the world….Social entrepreneurs have a unique approach that is both evolutionary and revolutionary, operating in free markets where success is measured not just in financial profit but also in the improvement of the quality of people's lives."

— Skoll Foundation

29. Crabs versus Turtles

Crab Mentality

This is an experiment you can do to learn more about crabs.

In many markets, crabs are sold in an open bucket, and there is no need for any covers as the crabs do not escape.

Whenever a crab tries to climb out of the bucket, other crabs will pull it down when it gets close to escaping.

"I can't have it, neither can you."

Crab mentality can manifest in many forms, and in many communities, they feel powerless and they get joy when they see others fail, and fear of failing prevents these communities from moving forward. There may be many problems that these communities face, but they do not work together to solve the problems.

Also known as 'crabs in a bucket', this is the kind of mindset that some communities have which prevents them to moving forward. It is far more common than you think. In Singapore, there is a term called "*kiasu*" which is prevalent in Singaporeans.

Kiasu or "fear of losing" is seen by some people as a positive thing. It makes Singapore a very competitive society, always trying to be the best in things. This mindset permeates through many different organizations in Singapore. It is often called a meritocracy society, where the top students in schools are on full government scholarships and groomed to be leaders. And these leaders are paid many times the average salaries of average Singaporeans, and are often placed in top positions in the government or government-linked companies.

emy   Kevin Chang   Alex
's insane."   "It's not enough that I should   "Yeah, su
                 succeed - others should fail."

This mindset has worked in building Singapore the way it is, but it also creates a lot of stress as everyone is very competitive. For some Singaporeans, success also means others should fail. This is the definition of crab mentality and it fragments a society and there is low public trust.

Turtle Mentality

Where crab mentality is not desirable, turtle mentality is positive (and adorable).

Baby turtles help each other dig out from a pile. The ones in the bottom push the ones on top upwards until everyone comes out. The process takes about an hour and no one is left behind.

This can also be observed among pet terrapins. These turtles will find ways to help their friends escape if the cover of their aquarium is not closed property and they can reach it. Through teamwork, these turtles climb on each other and push the one closest to the top and help him/her escape.

Many communities have very close relationships and support one another. In Japan, after the tsunami, the survivors self-organized their cleanup and shop owners on the street gathered every day to decide on which shops to clean up, allowing them to more efficiently clean the debris and mud rather than each shop owner cleaning their own store.

In Haiti, I've worked with Haiti partners and seen people in the village pooling money to send the children in their village to high school in Port-au-Prince. The people in the village also come together to apply for scholarships for all the eligible children and pool money to send them to universities.

Working together allows the villagers to accomplish tasks which may be difficult if a family were to do it alone. There are many examples of farmer cooperatives set up in rural villages to pool resources for bulk purchase and negotiate sales.

When working with communities, it is important to find ways to change their mindsets. It is not just having a solution that matters, but how the change can be sustainable. If the community has a crab mentality, the people you help may be pulled down again by others in the community and it is important to address these mindsets as well.

30. Risk versus Innovation

International NGOs (INGOs) have been around for many years working on the ground to provide clean water, improve education and alleviate poverty. The idea of empowering people means developing institutions which disempower themselves, however, one of the reasons why there is a huge challenge in having real impact is the fact that INGOs refuse to give up power and many have done little more than pay lip service to the sentiment.

Many INGOs are faced with questions and concerns about accountability and effectiveness. Scandals pop up from time to time causing media crises and sometimes making the INGOs move their headquarters to other countries. Some have even decentralized and others reshuffled their senior staff, but what exactly has changed?

The main problem with large INGOs is that most of them fail to take risks. Many of these INGOs have been set up years ago and have created systems for them to act fast and manage lot of people. With this comes a big bureaucracy and Standard Operating Procedures (SOPs). Over the years, when conditions changed with technology, norms and beliefs, patches were added on to a legacy system which became more and more cumbersome and less empowering for the staff. In many cases, things get so bad that nothing much gets done, and many systems are broken, but the organization continues to run in "autopilot mode" simply because of its size and reputation. Some of these organizations have toxic cultures which are sadly very risk averse and are afraid of anything new. Many of them talk about embracing innovation, but the culture does little to make it happen.

Large INGOs often fail to take risks and innovate. They simply pacify everyone because many of the senior managers are comfortable with business and the whole organization becomes less and less courageous.

The blame should not only go to these large INGOs. The large donors also demand control and many forms of "accountability" come from endless reports, which increase in complexity with every new project and collaboration.

The other paradox about empowering local communities is the fact that there is always a large pay discrepancy when it comes to salaries. Sadly, expatriate staff earn in magnitudes of the salaries a local person gets. In most companies, if two people who did the same role and had the same amount of experience got paid vastly different salaries, there would be uproar. Not so in the NGO world.

I have aid worker friends with their own stories of inequality in the workplace. Many local employees were paid less than half an expat's salary despite having both superior academic qualifications and experience.

I also have friends who work for INGOs and the ones working in operations on the ground in Haiti, Kenya and other field operation sites can easily receive less than half the salary of a manager in fundraising working in their office in Hong Kong or Singapore.

In terms of disaster recovery and rebuilding, a foreign consultant can easily get $3,000 a day, and when flown in for 10 days, their salaries can be a few times the annual salaries of a local consultant.

Hiring a foreign consultant for a high salary is usually not an effective way to spend funds, and when most of the funds are used on expat salaries, expat consultants and expat contractors, little is left to empower local staff who are stakeholders and who know the culture, history and environment better than the foreigners.

Since the managing staff are "not local", and they are paid exponentially more, hiring a highly skilled local in a third world country (who can do the job better) means taking the risk of putting the foreigners, whose salaries are paid via foreign donations, in a bad light, especially when the local who understands the local culture more wants to try out innovative solutions and create sustainable change.

I have started to see many changes happening. Many INGOs are starting to listen and engage with the local communities. They want to be involved with local projects. But in the end, INGOs still have the budgets and the power to decide what to do with what they have heard.

Many of these INGOs have big budgets, but sadly, most of this budget does not reach the ground or even local workers working for these INGOs.

With increasing frequency and magnitude of disasters, and an increasing number of people living in poverty, problems become more complex and require innovative ways to solve, by people with deep understanding of the root cause of the problems. And in the end, the solutions of these problems will probably not come from the large INGOs with all the resources, but from smaller local communities with innovation.

When a solution is found, is it more effective for the community to present the study in a report or simply be given more funds to scale up their solutions?

31. Never Help; Engage, Enable, Empower & Connect

Social intervention is a lot more complex than what people make it out to be. Over occasions such as Christmas, I see many people participate in giving. They donate money, warm clothes and many other things they do not need, and feel good about it.

I have asked a few of them when they donate about their stance on social welfare, minimum wage and redistribution of income. Consistent to my research, many of these people like giving, but do not like the idea of empowering others. They believe in the bootstrap theory where the poor should work harder and pull themselves out of poverty, and those who remain poor simply do not work hard enough.

Many people do not think it is a problem that there are people working full time, yet unable to support themselves and their families, because the wages are too low. They do not see the widening income gap causing more inequality. They think poor people are lazy and are not taking accountability for their actions.

After a few long discussions, my conclusion is that many people do not want to share power. They prefer to have all the power and give a little at a time under their total control. People feel they will lose power if they share it with others.

As far as the helping goes, much of the giving is for oneself to feel good, some give it out of pity, and others give to feel positive about themselves. As far as they are concerned, the impact of the giving is not important. They also do not care who it benefits and how it benefits the beneficiaries.

Giving has been going on for decades and few beneficiaries are now in a better position even after receiving aid for many years. This is because the current system of giving does not solve the root cause and people are content to continue to give.

This system is however not very sustainable. When the economy is bad, the giving stops while more people are in need of aid. The people requiring aid continue to require aid and it often form an endless cycle.

NGOs who want to continue their existence will continue to ask for donations and maintain status quo. They will show pitiful photos of human suffering to "guilt trip" people into giving. And over the years, the situation of those who suffer does not improve, it just remains the same.

So what can we do if we believe a change is needed? How can you contribute?

Never help; Engage, enable, empower and connect.

What I learned from my years working with different communities and groups of people is that poor people are not stupid, as is commonly perceived.

I have seen many innovative ideas come from marginalized communities. Locals from their communities understand their problems better than anyone else. The reason why a lot of solutions do not come from these communities is because of lack of resources to carry out the plan.

I co-founded Relief 2.0, a disaster relief organization during the Japan Tsunami in 2011. In Tohoku, we brought in a lot of ideas from the experiences we had from other disasters, but after engaging with the survivors in the shelters, we realized that most of the ideas worked only partially, and needed a lot of input from the locals to work completely.

Using the principles of engage, enable, empower and connect, we were able to support local communities using our design thinking and lean startup methodologies to immediate prototype solutions and quickly roll out successful processes.

Engage

You can try to design solutions for problems which do not exist. The solutions are not going to have much of an impact. Engaging the community you want to support is one of the most important steps which is generally overlooked.

Disasters happen all the time, and most people who have not experienced any disaster will simply think that other people will donate or that it is other people's problem. Without empathy, social problems like poverty, and lack of handicapped access seem to be "not my problem" and many people may think of donating just some money for the problem to go away.

The interns and volunteers who come to my recovery projects or empowerment workshops really felt that they needed to be part of the solution once they witnessed the conditions and met the marginalized people.

The fact is, people are thrown into these situations are sometimes just regular people until something bad happens, like a disaster. And sadly, I've also known many people living in poverty because someone in their family got into a serious health problem which drained away all their savings. When you start engaging with these real people, the problems seem much closer and people get deeply involved because of these engagements.

Engagement is also very important as the locals understand the environment, culture and problems they face — much better than anyone else. Before trying to formulate solutions without engaging, talk to the community and understand the needs on the ground.

A lot of problems are very complex and a solution proposed without consultation may not fix part of the problem and may not be their immediate need. It is like an old car that has engine problems. Changing the bald tires does not really solve the main problem.

Engagement is more than just talking. Many NGOs do tell their beneficiaries what to do and give them aid. Engaging is also not just taking orders from the community and giving them whatever they want. To engage is to communicate on an equal level, to learn to understand each other and discover ways to create value in the relationship.

Engaging the community also allows the community to participate in creating the solution. Many marginalized communities feel abandoned even when many people form solutions and are trying to solve their problems, just because there is no engagement with them at all.

A lot of times, these marginalized communities are made to feel that they are the problem. A better approach is to engage them and try to get them to be the solution to the problem that many other similar communities around the world face.

Engagement is not hard. Time is required to talk to various stakeholders to understand the current situation and what the main problems they may face are. Understanding the scope of the problem and the scale of the problem is very important and an engaged community can also participate in creating the solution. So you can get help from the community and they will work hard because they have vested interest. If the solution works, it solves their problems.

Just like the case of my chicken farm, getting the community engaged early allows them to "buy in" to the solution and make it their own, rather than being something from an external party.

Engagement also allows you to build relationship and trust. With a good communication channel, it is possible to monitor progress and impact as well. Good communications also create a deeper understanding of the situation to allow a more effective and efficient solution with community buy-in. And when things do not happen as expected, they can be communicated properly and resolved to ensure proper actions are taken to move in the right direction, rather than waste more funds and time doing things that have no impact on the ground.

Enable

When you solve all the problems for your child, he does not learn and cannot appreciate what is going on. When the same issues happen again, he will need your help again. The same thing happens when you help some people or a community.

The problems faced by marginalized communities usually occur over and over again. Unless you can continuously fix the problems every time they arise, would it not be better if they can solve the problems themselves?

One of the main reasons for the continuation of a lot of initiatives in these communities is the lack of resources. To solve some of the issues, they may need to have skills, equipment or even money. And in many cases, the non-profit organizations have these resources.

Instead of building homes for the survivors after a major earthquake, the survivors can be trained and given materials and equipment to design and rebuild their own homes. It would certainly cost less and they can learn new skills which they can use to get jobs.

Instead of providing food aid, teaching communities and providing them basic farming equipment would be more sustainable than continuously shipping in food to feed them indefinitely.

Many of these poor communities lack basic banking facilities, the knowledge to manage money, and entrepreneurial skills. They can be very creative and innovative, but without basic business knowledge and a little capital, it is hard for them to succeed if they can only afford to try once.

Social Entrepreneurship is a good way to enable marginalized communities as it can provide some of them jobs and a way to make a living. Many social enterprises work with disabled people, train them at the job and allow them to earn a living salary.

Knowledge also enables these marginalized communities to start their own businesses and find ways to solve their problem, and with advanced search engines, social media and the internet, the cost of access to knowledge is much reduced.

Technology is also advancing and with telemedicine, rural communities can have access to medical diagnosis to allow them to judge whether to send their sick or injured to the hospital or to allow them to rest and heal in the village.

These communities understand their problems and the local environment best, but as people from outside the community, what we bring along is our experience, skills, knowledge and diverse views which we can share to give them more options, to enable them to solve their problems.

Empower

It is important that after people learn how to solve their problems, they are actually allowed to solve them. In many cases, many non-profits come to these communities to help. And most of the time, the communities are not allowed to participate in creating the solution.

Organizations such as Habitat for Humanity will come into a community to rebuild damaged homes, but the locals living there usually do not participate in the planning and building process, and since the donors or volunteers who build these structures do not live there, they will build it according to how they think it should be like and their budget, rather than what is really needed.

When people are not empowered to solve the problem, they are sometimes seen as the problem. When the solution fails, they are also blamed for not trying. I have had my fair share of working on projects and not engaging locals, and have experienced much failure.

Now, I like to get the locals to buy in and work together on our (rather than *my*) solutions so they feel that they are part of the solution and are empowered to solve their pressing problems. They should be the ones most excited and they do have vested interest to see the success of the projects, and in time, they should be the ones in charge and running the project.[15]

Empowerment goes beyond help, it is an internal shift that results in a positive change in one's situation. Empowerment is not a quick fix. It is a process — a journey with ups and downs.

Empowering is something most people do not think of, but it is one of the most important steps towards equality. When Civil Innovation Lab (an overarching

---

[15] http://www.huffingtonpost.com/william-drayton/want-true-equality-make-e_b_9013242.html

organization of a series of transformative initiatives that I co-founded) runs lean startup bootcamps in Haiti and the Dominican Republic, and when the marginalized communities are engaged, many of them have lots of innovative business ideas and proceed to start their small businesses successfully.

Carlos Miranda Levy, co-founder of Civil Innovation Lab, even ran a lean startup workshop in the Najavo maximum security penitentiary, and the participants went on to create many interesting businesses which they started after they were released.

The problem is not with these marginalized communities — it's us. Society has created a negative environment and the environment that many of these communities are in is so poisonous that we keeping telling people "you can't".

Many young people in these communities keep hearing "you can't", and eventually give up and follow the conventional way of getting a low income job, taking up traditional farming and never trying to explore their dreams or ideas.

The mindset that you need a lot of money to start a business and that if you do not have an education, you will fail runs very strong in many communities, and as a society, we tend to just think of the people in the marginalized communities as "cheap unskilled labor", giving them skills training and fitting them into jobs, no matter whether they are suitable for them. We try to mold them in the image of how a poor villager should be like and they are never given a chance or trusted with the resources they need to succeed.

Trying to solve youth unemployment by "giving young people needed skills" is a chimera. In many cases, even access to education only leads to a generation of failures because much of the current education system is obsolete, and much of this education and training leads to low level jobs which are highly affected by the changing market needs.

The decision should not lie on a group of elites who decide who to "save" and how the problems should be solved, but rather, should involve having access to resources where everyone can solve their own problems. This way, everyone can take action and be responsible for their own well-being and success.

Empowerment means offering options. Marginalized communities do have dreams. When people are empowered, they can empower others. Empowering people changes mindsets and can catalyze a chain reaction. It enables a shift in power, from internal to social, from an individual to a community. Empowerment manifests itself where people express trust, belonging, spontaneity and creativity.

Connect

In many cases, the community may not have all the resources needed to completely solve their problems, but they may have a very viable solution which seems promising. Instead of providing all the resources needed, you can always connect the community to the right support they need.

There could situations where, for example, the government is already providing housing assistance for low income workers in the city and the marginalized community you are working with is trained with the right skills and have found a job, but are unable to afford rents. Instead of starting subsidized housing, connecting these workers with jobs and working with them through the bureaucracy to get them the subsidized housing would be just fine.

Most organizations cannot be good at everything, and most organizations cannot provide everything. The problems are often too complex for one department or organization to support, so connecting with other organizations is key.

This can also be done with crowdsourcing solutions. A community may have a small scale prototype which shows success, but with many other issues unresolved. It is ok if you don't have all the answers as well because you can always crowdsource solutions, funding and receive many other resources as well.

Today, with social media, a good initiative with a good story sells. Many people may want to get involved and they can provide far better resources than you. It is just a matter of connecting the dots and connecting the needs to the resources.

If there is a lack of funds, crowdfunding is now a viable option, and all you need is a smartphone and internet access to create a campaign to fund your projects.

32. Case Study 7: Amazon Disaster Registry

Over the course of my work, I have been to various disasters, setting up Relief 2.0 teams and projects to run the last mile of disaster relief. During Hurricane Sandy, I heard over the news that various parts of New York City and New Jersey were flooded.

I called up a few friends living in New York, and those who lived near flooded areas requested for laundry detergent and floor cleaner. I gathered some friends in Boston and requested for all their open bottles of detergents, and brought them to New York to pass to many people there.

Due to the flooding, many convenience stores and supermarkets were not open. After chatting with some of the people in the shelters and on the streets, though, I realized that many of them had access to vehicles and could get food from convenience stores outside the flooded areas, and others had enough food supplies in their homes. They were given mineral water and canned food, and for the majority of the city, tap water was still potable.

I met a group of volunteers on the ground and was introduced to the people from Occupy Relief Sandy. They were busy redistributing food to those who needed it. There was plenty of food in some shelters, but those trapped in their apartment building with eight feet of flood water beneath them did not have access to food.

I connected them to some other New York University (NYU) and Yale University students and they managed to consolidate some inflatable boats and kayaks to do the food delivery.

Chatting with the Occupy Relief Sandy group allowed me to share the needs of some people that I met on the streets and in the shelters. Those with babies could not find baby milk formula and diapers, however, such items were not provided by the NGOs and government shelters. We organized a Hackathon (a collaborative computer programming event) to try to solve the problem.

Within 24 hours of mobilizing programmers in various universities, a solution was created — The Amazon Disaster Registry. This registry allows anyone with a need (like flashlight, diapers, etc) to come to the booth and report their needs and their contact information. The volunteers would key it into the registry. While online, anyone interested in supporting those in need could buy the items for them.

This very tangible and efficient way of giving leaves nothing to waste. You get to buy what people need, you know what you spent your money on, and who gets it. The recipient gets what he needs, nothing more, nothing going to waste (maybe except the box it was shipped in).

There are a lot of innovative ways of doing things, but it takes a lot more effort than simply following status quo and donating money.

33. Case Study 8: Disaster Recovery through Art and Tourism

Basu Gautam (Founder of Lumbini World Peace Forum)

Lumbini World Peace Forum is partnering with Relief 2.0 on a project to run art exhibitions around the world. One of the goals is to raise awareness on the current rebuilding progress of Nepal, and another — using art to spread Nepalese culture to the world, selling art to raise funds to build art studios in the damaged villages, allowing the villagers to create handicrafts to increase their incomes to rebuild their homes.

This is a social initiative, targeting several different communities of people: Buddhists, Artists and the Social Innovators, to come and engage in an event where everyone can participate in empowering the survivors of the Nepal Earthquake to create arts and crafts to sell and use the funds to rebuild their homes.

Each show runs for a week and features more than 30 pieces of paintings, sculptures, Thangka (a traditional Buddhist form of painting) and Mithila (eye-catching folk paintings). This global show will display in Boston, New York, Los Angeles, Rosarito Beach and various parts of Europe.

Two prominent Nepali artists will be brought in to the show to share their knowledge on the Nepali art and how art can be used for social good. They will share their knowledge on Nepali art and their passion for Buddhism in their art. They will share experiences on how the earthquakes affect their art. And lastly, they will talk about why they feel the need to empower their communities to rebuild, and not just rely on the traditional donation model.

The art pieces' prices range from $150–$1,000 and we do a 20% profit sharing with the gallery spaces, which they may keep or use to support the next show as their CSR. The artists will get 20% of the sales for their time and costs, and the remainder after transportation and logistics will go towards building the residential art studios.

These studios can also house visiting artists who can stay and be inspired by Nepal's beautiful scenery. And the artists can create social art with the local villagers, and bring their experience back to their countries and promote Nepal as a tourist destination.

With more than 8,000 people killed and 2,000,000 people homeless after the twin earthquakes in Nepal in 2015, this project hopes to enable the survivors to earn more income to rebuild their own communities.

34. Case Study 9: Relief B2B (Business to Business)

The situation: about one month after the Japan Tsunami, the ongoing cleaning up is about to be completed in many towns. Some of the survivors are getting resettled in the temporary shelters and many of the survivors want to get their lives back to normal.

In Ishinomaki, a town badly hit by the tsunami, there were many buildings destroyed and many others damaged. The business owners have worked together to clean up their stores and the streets. Although most of the affected stores are cleaned up and boarded up by wood, the business owners have yet to open their stores.

After much engagement with these business owners, a few of them have decided to retire, some of them want to leave town and move in with relatives as they have lost everything. However, many others want to restart their businesses. A big barrier preventing them from restarting is actually access to loans.

Relief 2.0 has proposed several ideas, largely consisting of using the internet to get micro loans for the businesses to restart. After speaking to many of these business owners, the idea was rejected.

"Japan is a strong country. We can find a way to solve this problem without asking for international help."

The business owners want to restart, can't get loans and refuse international loans. Through much discussion to understand the culture and context, Relief 2.0 created Relief B2B, a bridging loan from other local business owners to those in the disaster areas who need loans to restart their businesses.

To start, we looked for businesses which are sole proprietorships. The businesses must be in buildings that are structurally sound and their loan amounts must be less than US$50,000. We asked the business owners about their situation, and if they just required a loan to restart their business, we would put them down as a candidate for Relief B2B.

Even when it was all planned out, there was much resistance as people generally do not want help from others, until you build trust with them. To ease their minds, we asked the business owners who wanted to restart their stores a few questions. "Do you buy your goods from your supplier and pay at the end of the month?" In most cases, the answer is "yes", because electrical bills, phone bills, etc are usually done in a form of credit. Establishing that they do understand that credit is part of business, we asked them if they were interested in getting interest bearing loans from local Japanese businesses willing to give them loans.

Most of them agreed, and although we did not guarantee we could get loans for them we shared our plans and processes for how we intended to get these direct loans and what they needed to do. We found a florist, a café and a bicycle shop who were interested to participate.

We interviewed the business owners in their cleaned up stores and asked them four basic questions and recorded them on video.

> "What happened during the disaster?"
>
> "What did you lose?"
>
> "How much do you need?"
>
> "What are you going to use the money for?"

After editing the video, we invited business owners from the neighboring town to gather and watch these videos. The business owners from the next town may have felt the same disaster, but they were affected to a much lesser extent. Most of them wanted to help but did not know how.

In the events that we ran, we instructed the business owners in other towns to bring their cheque books, but we were not asking for donations, but rather, interest bearing loans. After explaining the concept to them, we showed the videos of the survivors and their businesses, and had contracts drafted by pro-bono lawyers to give to the businesses who wanted to support.

The support we received was overwhelming. From two towns that we visited, we managed to raise the whole amount needed for the three businesses who wanted to restart. We would pass them the cheques and the contracts and they would sign the contact and mail a copy back to the business who loaned them the money.

Some people ask, "Why loans?"

At Relief 2.0, we believe that there are many needs after a disaster, and for the area to recover, economic recovery must happen. It is important for these small businesses to restart as they form the bulk of employment.

The business owners get income, their employees get paid, and they can get on to rebuilding their homes without begging. The interest for the loan is put in place so that the businesses do not ask for too much, since all the money they ask for must be paid back with interest.

Relief B2B is a model which allowed the town to recover economically without delay, and the survivors to make a living with dignity.

35. Case Study 10: Relief B2V (Business to Village)

In 2015, Nepal had two terrible earthquakes that caused more than 8,000 fatalities, and two million people homeless. I was there a few days after the first earthquake and the situation was dire. There were still a lot of problems of getting aid into the land-locked country, and a lot of the aid donated to Nepal was still at the airport customs waiting to be cleared.

There was a lot of damage on the UNESCO sites, and a couple of buildings collapsed, but overall, in comparison to the Asian Tsunami or the Japan Tsunami, I was a little relieved that the scale of devastation was not that high.

I connected a few of the different groups of people I know to form a Relief 2.0 team on the field and we ran the last mile of disaster relief, connecting the needs to the resources, and sourcing them if they could not be found locally.

A month later after the second earthquake, I returned to Nepal in hopes of running Relief B2B, however, I was pleasantly surprised when the people I met a month ago invited me to a restaurant in Thamel (a tourist district) for lunch, and most of the businesses had opened as normal.

We set up many trips to visit the damaged villages and spoke to the various business associations. Many villages were still in disrepair, and many of the businesses in Kathmandu were up and running. I realized that there was no need to run Relief B2B and that the focus should be on the villages.

A few problem-solving workshops were run in various villages, to find out more about the problems they were facing, and ways to solve them. After several days of brainstorming with a few villages they concluded that they need to address the lack of an ambulance. A few villages that were crushed by the collapsed buildings did not survive because there were no cars passing through the mountainous roads for hours after the earthquake.

There were further discussions on the need and the role of the ambulance, and the final conclusion was that they needed a van — a vehicle in which they could carry the injured to the hospital, but in other times, carry their harvest to the market.

The question was, how should they get this van? Should they save up and get it after several harvests? Or could they take a loan?

The problem faced by many of the people in the poor villages is, many things cost much more for poor people than other people, and one of them is loans. Poor people tend to pay higher interest rates.

Using the same assumptions that businesses are interested to help, I shared the idea of the villages needing a van to the businesses in the city, emphasizing that they did not need pity or donations. They needed access to low interest loans.

Speaking with the fast food association and restaurant association, they were interested to try out this business model and a pro-bono lawyer would draft out a contract to fix the prices of the harvest. The associations would pay for the van for the village cooperative to own, and the village cooperative would repay the loan with produce from their harvest.

Cutting out the middleman, the villagers earn much more and have direct access to the market, hence can repay their loans faster. If the fast food association wants to help or the restaurant association wants to help, giving the low interest loan allows the villagers to get the van immediately, and it also lets the association know the source of their food. Hopefully, this partnership can continue after the loan is paid and the villagers can earn more money.

36. Case Study 11: Relief Enterprise

After a disaster, Relief B2B supports business owners and their employees to restart their businesses.

However, business owners who have lost their homes and jobs because of the disaster still need continuous support. Relief Enterprise addresses this need.

Exclusion of Local Resources and Alienation of Funds

Natural disasters disrupt the economy and generation of wealth where they occur. It takes time for the economy to recover and most incoming resources for recovery are managed by foreign organizations, professionals and volunteers, excluding local stakeholders.

Funds provided by the international community are largely spent on foreign resources and remain outside the local ecosystem. Furthermore, local resources and stakeholders are not actively engaged in the relief and recovery initiatives, often being displaced by foreign providers and ending up depending on foreign aid, assistance and hand outs.

Lack of Sustainability and Transparency of Donation-based Relief and Recovery Initiatives

Nobel Peace Laureate Professor Muhammad Yunus teaches us that a donation dollar has a single life, from donor to beneficiary, while a social business investment dollar has infinite life because it generates profit which can be reinvested in the recovery and social initiative indefinitely.

Hundreds of thousands of people are affected every year by natural disasters and in response billions of dollars are spent every year in charity, but donors are become increasingly worried about the use, destiny and impact of their donations.

Transforming Donors into Conscious Consumers, Donation Recipients to Generators of Wealth

Relief 2.0 Marketplace allows those interested in helping disaster areas to buy goods from survivors or to employ them and get something back instead of making donations whose destiny is uncertain. You are not just helping with money, but enabling the survivors to engage in a sustainable, profitable and dignified activity. By combining multiple disaster areas, we become a diverse channel to connect them with a global audience of consumers interested in acquiring goods and helping at the same time.

An Entrepreneurial Approach to Disaster Recovery

Relief 2.0 Enterprise consists of three *enabling systems* to connect local stakeholders with a global market, and improve the capacity of *local resources*.

- *Relief 2.0 Marketplace:* A global on-line store of goods and services produced locally in disasters areas and offered to a global audience.

- *Relief 2.0 Match:* A global database and matching service of *local goods and services providers* and *requirements by international organizations*, supported by…

- *Relief 2.0 Skills:* A capacity building and certification program, which empowers local stakeholders and makes sure they match and meet the expectations of relief, local and international organizations.

Local Strategy and Participation of Local and Grassroots Organizations

Working together with local and community organizations and putting them in charge of local operations, we delegate the processes of: scouting for artisans, makers of goods and local service providers; contact with them; capacity building; and their certification.

The local partner organizations receive training and a support kit for training, evaluating and certifying local goods and service providers. They also cover the costs of the local operation, including web connectivity, phone services, local financial costs (incorporation, bank accounts), collecting goods to be shipped and distributing payments to the local providers. In exchange, they earn a percentage of the revenue.

A Proven Business Concept

Ours is a proven business concept that works. We are extending the impact and reach of the fair trade and community engagement models and applying it to disaster areas and survivors.

Unique and Special Marketplace

Complete traceability of funds, accountability and transparency of operations

Buyers know exactly where their money goes, how it is distributed and which community, artist, professional or seller gets the money and what percentage of it.

Engagement of communities impacted by disasters

We focus on communities affected by disaster and boosting their recovery through the activation of the local economy and generation and distribution of local wealth.

Promoting social entrepreneurship, sustainable and dignified activities

Beneficiaries' income is based on the amount of sales, not a fixed income, donation or salary.

This allows them to become entrepreneurs, hire others, distribute costs and expand.

Customized, on-demand products

Users can pay a premium price to request personalized items customized by the artists (songs with the buyer's name in the lyrics, stories with the name of a child included in the book or audio, paintings with a desired theme, embroidered initials on clothing, etc.).

Stakeholder-centered approach: Direct/personal connection with beneficiaries

Every community, business, artisan, producer and store participating gets its own space to showcase their information, products and updates through stories, pictures and videos and through which they can be contacted directly.

All information and product information is updated directly by sellers or their representatives.

A social business model

Relief 2.0 Marketplace is a business created with a social purpose. It operates efficiently with a business model to generate profit. However, *Relief 2.0 Marketplace* does not pay dividends to its owners or investors. All profit is reinvested in the project or spent to strengthen the local capacity of the stakeholders we aim to serve.

We strictly follow the Social Business Model defined by Nobel Laureate Prof. Muhammad Yunus and the Grameen Creative Labs around the world. Donors, investors and sponsors of *Relief 2.0 Marketplace* can expect and agree to receive the full amount of their investment back after an agreed period of time, but never more than what they have invested.

Volunteer and Pro-bono Coverage of Expenses

We keep our operation costs low by leveraging the power of volunteers and partners who cover most of the expenses offering pro-bono services:

- Volunteers and partner community and grassroots organizations coordinate the participation of local sellers, their product information, stories and their order fulfillment processes.

- Impact Foundation Japan absorbs the administrative and legal fees, adopting Relief 2.0 Marketplace as a project running under its legal structure.

- Grameen Creative Lab provides support, mentoring and advice on legal and operative structure and logistics.

- CIVILA.com, Doing.gd and Relief 2.0 provide the servers, programming, design, platform development, hosting, etc.

Many problems are part of a complex adaptive ecosystem. "Outsiders" have difficulty understanding the system, hurting their ability to create sustainable solutions.

In Boston, high school graduation rates are relatively high and drop out rates are much better than the national average. The quality of education in Boston is very good and the school committee does a lot to share best practices, even having trainers from charter schools help out in the public system. Despite using all the best innovation, technology and processes similar to those in charter schools, in 2013, the dropout rate in Boston Day and Evening Academy (BDEA) was 30.7%, much higher than the national average of under 7%. Dropout rates may seem like an education problem, but using just an academic solution (better ways of teaching) sometimes does not solve the root problems, which may be related to housing and school access.

On the flipside of this, a project in Kenya that gave kids free uniforms, textbooks, and classroom materials increased enrollment by 50%, but this swamped the teachers and reduced the quality of education for everyone.

There also is the complexity of self-sabotage. Communities in India cut off their own water supply so they could be classified as "slums" and be eligible for slum-upgrading funding. I've worked in places where as soon as a company sets up a health clinic or an education program, the local government disappears — why should the government spend money when a rich company is ready to take on the responsibility?

We may think that the system is broken, that it is hopeless, and that nothing can be done. After years of research to end poverty, there are more people in poverty than before. What actually may be wrong are our expectations.

We want things fast, cheap and good. Social enterprises that demonstrate competency often try to quickly scale. The results are always "success, scale, fail". There are unreasonable expectations on how fast the organization should grow once it receives funding. While you may have run a project successfully, scaling up 50 others is not so straightforward.

When we support a social enterprise, we should not expect miracles to happen overnight. Even charities need to pay people a fair market rate to retain talent, otherwise you either get people who cannot get jobs elsewhere or job hoppers. Simple numbers like overheads or number of programs don't effectively compare different social enterprises or charities. Numbers, charts and graphs do not tell the full story on the ground.

Society equates helping with donations, so there is outrage when there are overheads involved in running charities, foundations and social enterprises. We understand the concept "Feed a boy a fish, he eats for a day. Teach a boy to fish, he eats for a lifetime." However society still takes pity on the marginalized communities, continuously providing food and medical supplies. Billions upon billions of dollars have been poured into so many organizations, yet the areas they serve often are in no better shape years later than when they were first presented. Why is poverty only getting worse?

Conscious Consumerism — The Needed Change

We need to fundamentally change the way people give. Giving out of pity removes all dignity in receiving the aid. Instead, looking at and investing in people's potential to get themselves out of poverty should be the key to solving the problem.

Next, say "no" to sensationalism. Many charities like to create emotionally driven ads that often distort the truth to push a point across. Empathy should be the standard emotion on which relationships are built. The focus should be kept on what is possible instead of the plight of the situation which usually brings much shame to the recipients of the donations.

Conscious consumerism can replace donations. When you donate, the money is being used once for food or necessities. When you support a business, you support the community and others in a more sustainable way. When there is a disaster, support local business in the disaster area when they are rebuilding as any amount, however little, does help.

We need to believe in the hidden potential of the people we want to help. Stop thinking of people as "needy", "handicapped" and "pitiful". Instead, look at them as people who need to be engaged and empowered with skills to solve their own problems. Enabling them to think positively while connecting them to the relevant help they need creates a positive path to where they can be productive in society and get their dignity back.

Challenges to Conscious Consumerism

Conscious consumerism is not a new concept. Today, many shoppers look to purchase products that are healthier, more environmentally friendly, and in some cases, driven towards generating community impact.[16] Many younger people are driving this with a belief — "when you shop, you are casting a vote in the type of world you want to live in".

I've worked on Relief 2.0 Marketplace and various other initiatives to drive conscious buying and here are some lessons I learnt.

[16] Nielsen's Global Survey on Corporate Social Responsibility states that "55 percent of global online consumers are willing to pay more for products and services provided by companies that are committed to positive social and environmental impact." http://www.sustainablebrands.com/news_and_views/stakeholder_trends_insights/aarthi_rayapura/new_nielsen_study_says_consumers_are_read

(a) Many consumers say that they are willing to pay more for products and services provided by companies that are committed to positive social and environmental impact — but some actually don't do it.

It is hard to change the behavior of the consumer. They are bombarded by advertisements online, offline and on TV. At the end of the day, quality and price matters. There are a lot of talks on sustainability, but for someone living in a first world country, they do not get to see how the waste is managed and how pollutants affect agriculture and livestock. And in the end, they fall back to their consuming pattern.

Nielsen data also shows that only 15% of Canadian households purchase 100% recycled products. The reason is that consumers almost always go for price and quality first, not social impact.

This means that the conscious product needs to be:

(1) Competitively priced.

(2) Of comparative quality.

(3) Well communicated. (With good marketing and awareness campaigns.)

(4) Accessible and easy to buy.

The social purpose must also appeal to a wide enough base to build a strong and loyal customer base.

(b) Consumers are still wary of social intent and unsure about social impact.

Many consumers still do not know about conscious consumerism and think that the best way is still donating to charity. The deep rooted charity mindset and model suggests that business and social impact cannot co-exist.

The reality today is that many global businesses are in fact scalable and creating great social impact.

- Grameen Danone — a social-impact collaboration between Danone and Grameen Bank — makes a nutritious yogurt packed with nutrients to combat malnutrition in the developing world.

- LOHAS — Lifestyles of Health and Sustainability — is an industry with various brands with sustainable fashion, and fair trade sourced organic products.

The power of conscious consumerism will continue to grow and this billion-dollar segment will play a major role in the economy. As long as the product is great, the social purpose is sincere and the impact is real, consumers will choose to buy these products if the price is reasonable.

This is definitely a trend that is growing as businesses and consumers realize that business and social impact can go hand in hand and that there is an alternative to charity for social impact.

37. Human-Centric Community Empowerment

Have you been to Disneyland or Universal Studios? How was the experience? For children, Disneyland is a place where they can experience their favorite cartoon characters. They have been doing it for years: when my parents were kids, they would watch Mickey Mouse on TV and even today's kids know about Mickey Mouse, without ever watching the cartoon on TV.

What is so special about the experience in Disneyland? Firstly, you are brought into a surreal environment and there is a whole ecosystem built to enchant the children, while importantly, allowing parents to become heroes for having taken their kids there. It continues to evolve, and after buying the Star Wars franchise, you get to meet Kylo Ren and the other *The Force Awakens* characters at Disney Parks to further the story. As such, Disney is not just selling you products or a movie. They are selling an experience.

Disneyland resorts and parks created a wearable computer bracelet that provides consumers with the seamless ability to purchase without cash, review waiting times at rides, book FastPasses, open hotel room doors, get in and out of parks, and make dinner reservations. The customer relationship management (CRM) system used by the hotels also gives you promotions based on your activity, location and preference. Engaging consumers just enough so that they can increase loyalty and operational efficiency.

You can read up about the value of offering customers superior customer experience. Apple has shown us this when they launched the iPhone in 2007 and its rich experience ecosystem, built right into the product. Many companies try to copy what Apple has done, but so far, none have really done it well. Apple has clearly demonstrated that consumers will pay a premium for a better experience even when they may just have a regular product.

For companies, the experience architecture is the art of engendering desired emotions, outcomes, and capabilities throughout the customer journey. It is the process of designing and strengthening the whole spectrum of the customer's experience strategically through every single interaction with the company.

Customers have demands not only on good products and services, but on the ongoing experience as well. In a way, experiences are more important than the product itself. With social media, th_s has also become a topic which is shared in our connected economy. Businesses can nurture desired experience or react to/make up for bad experiences.

So What can we Learn from Businesses?

Top businesses evolve and strive to be on top and we can learn a lot from them. One key takeaway is creating positive engagement and experience through every interaction. If customers are just treated as any other customer, the experience will not be great, and at the same time, when you are interested in supporting individuals to empower a community, the engagement needs to be customized and unique to that community. The experience can in turn change behaviors, build trust and create a sustainable buy-in by the community.

In a sense, the ideas and solutions you create for a community may be good, but the experience and engagement eventually will be more important than the idea itself. Good experiences gain support and start creating positive behavioral change. Bad experiences push these communities away.

How do you create a positive experience? Technology tweaking and social media do not constitute experience architecture.

A good community experience is **not**:

- A campaign,
- Online crowdsourcing,
- Raising funds to build something,
- Online fundraising,
- An app,
- A tagline,
- Understanding SEO,
- Knowing how to use good design and colors,
- Hackathons…
- Anything other than implicit and explicit design, engagement, reinforcement and shaping of meaningful and sharable experiences — ALL THE TIME.

> **Example:**
>
> A good car salesman does not sell you the features of the car, the warranty and brand of the vehicle. He sells you the car for YOU. He tells you what you want to hear to get the sales done, and makes the purchase experience as positive and simple as it can be.

Working with different disaster communities, I realized that everyone's needs are different. It is important to support the basic human needs like food, shelter and clean water, however, there are many other human needs which are not provided.

Human-centric Disaster Relief

Who are the survivors in a disaster?

They are doctors, mothers, engineers, teachers... Disasters destroy the physical infrastructure, but the social structure remains. Disasters do not destroy capacity or knowledge.

From my previous experience in other disaster areas, I have seen and have been guilty of exclusion and displacement. If there is a task to be done, it is always possible that a local will be present who can do a better job.

> **Example:**
>
> Large NGOs running a shelter use volunteers, with a bulk of them students; they perform tasks like cooking and distribution of food. Although the survivors do get food, the quality of the food is always questionable.
>
> After the Japan Tsunami, I was in Ishinomaki with a Relief 2.0 team. Like in all other disasters, the survivors were staying in the assigned shelters and there were many volunteers helping. When I was visiting the shelters to find out more information on the current needs, during lunch and dinner, I saw many volunteers busily preparing the meals. As I had left my meal in another shelter, I waited for everyone to have their dinner and I got mine after everyone else. The food was rather bland and when I talked to the young college-aged volunteers who prepared the meals, I learnt that most of them do not normally cook on their own. The next day, I called for volunteers among the survivors. Are there any professional chefs? Are there mothers who can prepare food for many people?" I saw several volunteers put up their hands. I had a short chat and asked them if they would be interested to cook for the shelter if they were allowed to and if they would do a better job. The answer was yes.
>
> Talking to the shelter manager, I asked him if the survivors who were professional chefs or mothers could volunteer to cook dinner while the other present staff chefs could support. The manager allowed the survivors to participate in the cooking and the result was much tastier food for everyone. The survivors also felt empowered to do something for the community.

Empowerment goes beyond help. Empowering survivors to work on a solution to better their situation, giving them an opportunity to contribute in a positive way is important to their mental well-being. Doing everything for the survivors makes them feel powerless and helpless, and it increases the chance of depression in the community.

Example: Donating used clothes after a disaster.

Many people donate clothes after a disaster. However, most NGOs will tell people not to donate clothes as the survivors don't take them. But when survivors lose their homes and are left with just what they have on, there is a definite need for clothes.

The NGOs are not lying, but it is a half truth. I have been to many shelters after a disaster and I do see lots of boxes of donated clothes unopened all the time. I found it puzzling initially when I saw people who had only one set of clothes not taking the free donated clothes. However, in Japan, after I tore a pair of my jeans, I decided to check the donated clothes and realized one thing. When the boxes of free clothes are stacked up so high and are unopened, it feels hazardous and too much work to sort through the clothes to find the size I need.

I am sure the survivors felt the same way as well. Anyway, torn jeans do not kill you and I decided not to get the jeans.

I informed a friend and he immediately took action. I brought a bag of candy and we gathered the kids in the shelter and requested for their help. If they could help us sort the clothes according to size, I would share my bag of candy with them.

The kids were very excited and the roll of nylon rope was put to good use. We tied the ropes to the windows and pillars and the kids hung the clothes on the hangers neatly according to size, color and type. At the end of the day, all the clothes were sorted, the kids had fun and now had candy.

I managed to find a pair of jeans in my size and over the next few days, more than half of the donated clothes were taken.

When NGOs tell you not to donate clothes, it means they do not have the capacity to sort the clothes in a way that the survivors can make use of them. It does not mean that the survivors do not need clothes.

Disasters destroy the physical infrastructure, but the social infrastructure remains. Disasters do not destroy capacity or knowledge. Disasters don't create refugees, they create survivors. It is the conventional relief system that turns survivors into refugees.

Relief 2.0 is the practice of running the last mile in the field through independent field units supported by mobile technologies and social networks, connecting resources, stakeholders, needs, organizations, volunteers and survivors in an efficient, effective and timely manner, filling the gaps created by bureaucracy and slow response from top-down hierarchies.

It is the result of field experience, the relentless pursuit of committed volunteers to be effective and respond to the requests of disaster survivors and the humane sympathy and empathy of global volunteers who remotely support their operation using mobile phones, community radio, the internet and social media and networks.

Relief 2.0 deploys multidisciplinary and mixed small independent units of locals and foreigners, empowered to assess each situation and make decisions on their own, constantly connected and supported by mobile technologies and a distributed network of contacts which monitors and follows their activities and requests via mobile phones, SMS, twitter feeds, blogs and social networks and relays any needs they have to others who can in turn relay to others until the needs are fulfilled by someone in a broad network of volunteers, stakeholders and concerned institutions.

As opposed to top-down, rigid chains of command and action, these units form a distributed open network where each member has connections in multiple directions and is willing to hook up to other networks. When confronted with a problem, each unit solves it with self-initiative without waiting to be told what to do, and when unable to do so, relays the need and enables others to help.

Example: Need for Tampons.

In Ishinomaki, after the tsunami, I saw many teenage girls helping with the cleanup work. A few days after I arrived, the all the teenage girls seemed to stay in the shelters while the teenage boys were still outside helping with the cleanup. The condition outside was nasty, the weather was cold and mud was everywhere.

I was not sure if the girls were just lazy and so I asked some of them in the shelters. Most of them were too shy to talk about it until one of the teenage girls informed me about menstrual synchrony — all the girls were having periods at the same time. I did not know such a thing existed until then.

Since all the stores were closed and the NGOs did not provide tampons, none of the girls wanted to be active. Coupled with the lack of running water, the girls did not want to get blood stains on their pants.

Relief 2.0 informed everyone coming to Ishinomaki to buy all the tampons they could find while Relief 2.0 ran an online campaign to crowdfund the reimbursement for the tampons. More than 1,000 tampons were distributed and more than 90% of the costs incurred were supported by the community.

The next day, the teenage girls were out helping with the clean up again.

Like the case where Relief 2.0 supported Occupy Sandy Relief, engaging the locals to solve their needs or empowering them to solve problems with tangible giving to fill gaps on the ground is important. It can also be carried out with haste and without delay using modern mobile networks and social media.

---

38. Social Capital

What is Social Capital?

Social capital refers to the collective value of all "social networks" [who people know] and the inclinations that arise from these networks to do things for each other ["norms of reciprocity"]. (Harvard Kennedy School)

Social capital is a form of economic and cultural capital in which social networks are central, transactions are marked by reciprocity, trust, and cooperation, and market agents produce goods and services not mainly for themselves, but for a common good. (Wikipedia)

Design is a fundamental creative problem solving process through which the highest potential of innovation for the benefit of humankind — and ultimately, a better world — may be realized. (Steve Jennings)

How does Social Capital Work?

Social Capital creates value for people who are connected and for others in the community. It focuses on not just the "feeling good" part of giving, but also builds trust, reciprocity, information and other cooperation and collaboration with the social networks.

Building your social capital is great when it comes to solving a social problem. The "connections" from the "weak ties" are essential to get resources your close networks do not have access to.

The Importance of "Weak Ties"

Everyone has strong bonds with close friends and "Weak Ties". The "Weak Ties" can be your bosses, alumni, lecturers, mentors, and various others you may be connected with on LinkedIn. As you may know, you share many similar friends or resources with your close friends. When you lack a certain resource, like when you want to change a line of job from being an electrical engineer to running a Green Startup, your close friends may not have the right contacts as they may also be engineers and do not know anyone in the sustainable industry. However, you may have others in your "Weak Ties" network that may be able to connect you to the people that may help you.

Connections are very important in social innovation. This is especially true when the same problem spans several countries. Due to the difference in cultures and experience, many countries may have different solutions to the same problem. This allows you to have different options to share when tackling the problem.

Example:

During the Japan Tsunami, I wanted to contact a person on the ground to find out more about the ground situation from a local rather than rely on news that was coming out. Going through my Facebook friend list, I called several friends in Japan and managed to contact someone in Sendai. He lives in Sendai city and he informed me that the Japanese army, Red Cross and numerous other NGOs were there, and there were absolutely no other needs as they had power and running water. He informed me that most of the damage was up north, and so I had to dig deep into my other contacts to try to speak with someone.

After contacting the various alumni groups that I know, calling friends of friends and other acquaintances, I managed to get someone who had been to Ishinomaki and I got connected to the mayor who informed me that they had had no power, running water or fuel for heating for more than five days, but that the Japanese army would be arriving in two days. I asked what sort of aid would help and he said that this was his first large scale disaster as a mayor and he may need some people who can manage logistics, and he got us permits to go on the highway to get to Ishinomaki.

If it was just my close friends, even with many friends in NGOs and foundations which deal directly with disaster relief and recovery, I would not have connected and gone to Ishinomaki where a lot of needs were unmet. I probably would have ended up in Sendai like many other NGOs, over-serving the population of survivors as no one else was allowed to go up north because the Japanese army wanted to coordinate the recovery effort centrally.

In Ishinomaki, when I found out an unmet need, the lack of tampons, I shared the problem on various outlets of my social media and managed to get some doctors who were coming up to Ishinomaki to buy the tampons on their way up.[17]

Many people build their net worth, they pay to attend classes to learn to invest and make passive income. Many people will spend most of their time making money, and finding ways to earn and save more.

---

[17] As an aside, according to Elizabeth Scharpf, Founder and Chief Instigating Officer, Sustainable Health Enterprises (SHE):

Millions of girls and women in developing countries miss up to 50 days of school/work per year because they do not have access to affordable sanitary pads when they menstruate. Currently, girls and women in this setting — if they have an option at all — turn to premium priced international brands which are too costly to sustain (e.g., in Rwanda, of the girls who miss school, 36% of them miss because pads are too expensive). Alternatively, they turn to rags which, in combination with a lack of a clean accessible water supply, are unhygienic and potentially harmful, let alone ineffective to contain leakage.

I know many people living the classic "work hard play hard" lifestyle. But it turns out that's a horribly inefficient way to get enjoyment out of life. Unless you truly love your job, the "work hard" part means you're losing out on a lot of time when you could be doing something you care about. And the "play hard" part winds up feeling empty, because you're trying to compensate for all that lost time.

At one time, I had built up my net worth and had many acquaintances working on property development and other business investments projects. However, when my father passed away and one of my companies because insolvent and I had my father's medical bills to worry about, many of my business acquaintances who focused on net worth were nowhere to be seen. The only people who stood by my side were my real friends, many of them did not have the capability to help me in my financial situation, but even when they were not well off, they offered to give me loans.

That was what drove me to build my social capital and not focus on net worth, as you may never know what kind of help you may need, and not every problem you have can be solved with money.

39. Circular Economy

The circular economy is a generic term for an industrial economy that is producing no waste and pollution, by design or intention, and in which material flows are of two types, biological nutrients, designed to reenter the biosphere safely, and technical nutrients, which are designed to circulate at high quality in the production system without entering the biosphere. (Wikipedia)

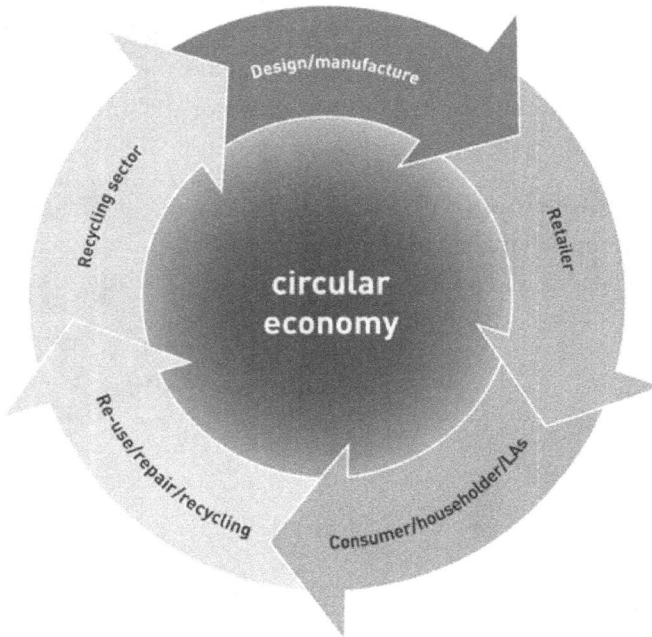

When designing solutions, you may want to consider using the circular economy. Currently, our linear economy way of 'make, use and dispose' is not sustainable and relies on large quantities of cheap, easily accessible energy and materials. You may consider making products with a lower price to compete in this highly competitive marketplace, but in the long run, it exploits resources and creates waste, all in which is detrimental to the community.

At the same time when you are considering social innovation and new opportunities, considering a more circular economy will:

- Reduce waste

- Drive better resource productivity

- Reduce environmental impacts on production and consumption
- Address resource scarcity/security issues
- Rebuild capital — financial, manufactured, human, social or natural

Why Circular Economy is Important

We have a finite world with finite resources. The current way we manage resources is linear, where we buy products, discard the packaging, use the product, and discard it when it is less functional than before. Today, in many cities, people don't even think about repairing their TVs, fans and other electrical appliances. These appliances do not last as long as before, and get discarded sometimes when a newer version comes out.

Today, there are more and more people living in the cities and you can see this as more of a challenge. When we look at the cities today in Asia, there are large sprawls and growth in both population and resource consumption. The linear way that we consume in the world of finite resources is not sustainable. We are using up these resources faster than ever, how will that pan out to the future?

When you start looking at cities as a connected area, you can see that it is much easier to consolidate waste, biological materials and other resources. With a high population density, there are economy of scale, and there is much opportunity and potential. If packaging waste, human waste, farming waste and waste water can be recovered and fed back to the biosphere, you can turn that into energy and fertilizer for farms; you can treat waste water and recover potable water for flushing.

In a developed country, you can reconnect the system which generates fertilizer, water and energy, and the city now becomes a resource. This may bring the farms closer to the city, requiring less transportation, less refrigeration and less packaging.

By looking at the whole system of the economy, you can see how things are interrelated, and how we can have unintended consequences from one thing that we do. This principle can also be applied to charities, social enterprises and other social projects. While giving people things, we generate unintended consequences which we may not understand, and which may be hard to rectify.

If you look at the whole system, you start to think of how you can use resources which can be restorative and regenerative. Because on the way towards a circular restorative and regenerative economic model, making sense of stocks and flows is essential in order to foster effective use of resources, identify areas of brittleness, and rebuild capital where necessary.

Understanding these consequences will also allow us to see long term consequences. For the case of the Aral Sea,[18] human activities diverting water for irrigation cause the Aral Sea to dry up. And with much resource spent doing this, today, the farming activities have also been greatly reduced as the dry lands that were irrigated could not get enough water to support irrigation. The unintended consequences of this also include the destruction of a whole fishing economy and much environmental damage and problems in public health.

The system where the materials flow within, where resources like metal, plastic are recovered and fed back into the economy, simply delivers more value. The region, the cities and the consumers ultimately benefit from the circular system when proper design is done — resulting in less waste and less materials imported.

To consider a circular economy, here are a few tips:

Reduce

Consider using less packaging, less use of plastics and non-recyclables. Eliminate the concept of waste. Participate in systems to collect and recover the value of materials following their use. For products like food, having large quantities will reduce packaging, however the food waste will be increased if the products are not saved and used for future dishes. If the packaging comes in a container which can be reused, then the packaging will not be discarded once the product is removed.

If products can be made modular, allow mass customization to allow consumers to use what they need.

Renew

Maximize the use of renewable resources. Consider using solar energy, wind power and other renewable sources.

Consider using recycled products, possibly using parts which you can recover from your products at the end of life.

---

[18] https://en.wikipedia.org/wiki/Aral_Sea

For projects, consider getting the community to train within themselves to ensure that there are always enough people to do the job. When you have succeeded through the system, pay it forward.

Extend

Create a modular design to allow parts of the products to be replaced when damaged. This can extend the life of the product.

Ensure durability of products. Some added designs can make products last longer and thus reduce waste at the end of life.

Industrial Ecology

Create a closed loop system which may reduce or eliminate undesirable by-products. Understand the production process of all the components and create frameworks which reduce ecological impact. Focus on natural capital restoring and also social wellbeing.

Collect end-of-life products if possible and recycle components in production to reduce waste and resources. Understand and study the material and energy flow through the industrial system and design efficiently to lower cost and the use of resources.

40. Case Study 12: Prison Entrepreneurship

There is always spare capacity in a community. In marginalized communities, they may lack resources and money, but poor people are not stupid. They can come up with great solutions to fix the current problems, but due to the constant rejection and lack of resources, many of them give up trying.

Prison Entrepreneurship

Najayo Penitentiary in the Dominican Republic, previously like any other prison in Latin America, was overcrowded and corrupt. Inmates had to buy places to sleep, or sleep standing up. But in the last 10 years, there was a slow transformation to a more humane model. Officials said less than 5% of inmates released from the model system re-offend; in the traditional system the rate is 50%.

Being part of this transformation, Civil Innovation Lab was part of the entrepreneurship training program for prisoners, bringing lean startup methodologies from Silicon Valley to one of the most dangerous prisons in the Caribbean.

The system basically treats the prisoners as the humans they are and human rights are respected. With a whole change of staff where none of the new guards had experience with the military or police, there was no connection to the traditional model. In fact, education is compulsory in the prison and inmates can obtain bachelor's degrees in law or psychology.

Together with Carlos Miranda Levy, my co-founder at Civil Innovation Lab, we did workshops on entrepreneurship and social business, treating the inmates like any student we had taught at the various universities. I found that the inmates were respectful and genuinely interested, though skeptical at the start about the possibility of starting a business, let alone a business with a social cause.

But building a community of inmates, ex-prisoners who have succeeded and social innovators proved to be a sustainable way to reduce prison populations and cut recidivism rates. It was not easy to build trust, but we managed to find people who believed in the program and connected the prisoners with resources and created a safe environment where they could fail safely and learn from their experience. Most important is empowering them to make the change and listening to their ideas and believing that they will follow through and have what it takes in themselves to succeed.

I visited the prison with Carlos during the transformation, and the conditions of the "old" part of the prison were very bad and still overcrowded, but the "newer" part was clean and tidy. The prisoners that were part of the training were however very respectful, and eager to learn.

Our idea was to teach lean startup methodologies and social business to give the prisoners more options when they come out of prison. But before they come out, in the last six months, they can also plan to run a mockup of their business in prison to learn about managing people and their business model.

When they are ready to come out, these prisoners are connected to ex-prisoners who had become successful and given a small seed funding loan to start their business. These new entrepreneurs would still have to bootstrap their way to success, and hire other ex-prisoners in their company if possible, creating jobs in a country with high unemployment rates.

Lastly, these entrepreneurs will have to return to share their experiences, success or failures to other inmates in the system, so as to pay it forward and create a closed loop ecosystem where there will be continuous trainers and funding for the system without any support from any external parties.

Civil Innovation Lab has the support from the Dominican government as reducing recidivism rates does save a lot of money for the government, and it also allows these ex-prisoners to be resources to create more value for the country.

41. Case Study 13: Solar Forward

Following the Nepal Earthquake in 2015, many communities were left without power. However, even after a year, the power had not returned to these communities. Many NGOs had called for donations of solar kits to give some of these communities light. I met up with several of these groups and they were interested in giving a few hundred solar kits to villages, however, as there were millions living in the dark, the question I often asked is, "How do you pick who receives these solar kits?"

Looking at the projects and speaking to people from the villages, the feedback I received was that, there is a real need for light and cell phone charging. Having a few more hours of productivity, having energy to power lights and charge cell phones is very important indeed. The fact is, many of these communities do have a need to charge their phones for communication. Their children do go to school, and light is important for them to do homework. Some of the residents in the villages do have other work besides farming, and a few more hours of light could make them more productive.

I felt that access to sustainable energy is a basic human need. For a post disaster community, there will be NGOs to give food, water and shelter, but these communities also need sustainable energy. But when funding is limited, the question is who will receive these solar kits, and how do we make more people benefit eventually?

From the engagement with the various communities, I got to know that some of the farmers in the villages do have extra work on the side. These farmers are also tailors, cobblers and artisans. They work after the day ends, and a few more hours of light would mean extra income for them. This extra income would mean a big difference in terms of earnings, and they could now make more money and save up to rebuild their homes.

Solar Forward is a crowdsourced project that plans to raise funds to bring in 500 low cost solar kits, consisting of Solar Panels, LED bulbs and a charger which can store the energy and charge cell phones. The local team in Nepal will curate 500 people from the various villages damaged by the earthquake, and give them these solar kits. The criterion for the curation is how much more these communities would make if they were given a solar kit.

If the family would earn at least US$1 more per day, just by having four more hours of light, and they would save the extra $1 a day, in 60 days, they would have US$60, which could buy another kit for someone else in their village.

If this family would agree to save up and buy another kit to benefit someone else in the village that would have financial gains when they receive the kit, they would be a potential candidate to receive the solar kit. This is testing a pay-it-forward model, which transforms the victim of an earthquake from a passive receiver of aid, to an active participant in the recovery process, empowering them to support others in their villages.

Working with Nepal Innovation Lab, studies on success or failure of the project, and how the community reacts to the pay-it-forward model will be studied and the results shared.

There is also a concern for those who do need the solar kit, but cannot commit to saving an extra US$1 a day. Many families could however, save up US$0.30–US$0.50 a day. These families would be part of the second phase of the Solar Forward project. Once the initial 500 solar panels arrive, the cost of shipping, customs clearance would be confirmed. And we can have the exact price of each of these panels delivered to Nepal.

The local Nepal team is also now looking at finding foundations and various institutions to be bank guarantors. As the communities are out of the banking system, it is very hard for them to get a US$50 loan for the solar kit. Having a bank guarantor would allow them to access the bank loan. And after building credit by paying off the loans, these communities could be integrated back into the banking system and have access to more loans.

The initial calculations show that they can pay a US$50 loan in as little as seven months if they save US$0.30 a day. And the other benefit would be that after paying off the loan, the communities could also build up a credit history for them to have access to the banking system.

Lastly, for those who may not even save US$0.30 a day, they can also access microfinance, which will train them in running a business or other skills which will help them generate income and the microfinance companies could them put them on a microfinance loan, allowing them access to solar energy.

This project is still ongoing, and the results will be made available once the project is completed.

42. Case Study 14: The Sustainability Place Of Destiny ("SPOD")

Development of Future Youth Leaders

Tay Kok Chin (Founder, Global SEnSE) and James Tian (GM, Red Shield Industry)

The Need for Sustainability Globally

The news on 3rd August 2015 that the water levels at the Linggiu Reservoir in Johor (Malaysia) were at about 55% of normal levels should be a matter of concern for Singaporeans.[19] Then Singapore Minister for the Environment and Water Resources, Dr Vivian Balakrishnan said this was "unprecedented" since the reservoir started its operations in 1995. More recently, on 13th November 2015, it hit record low level.[20]

Air pollution in many cities around the world has posed health risks, so much so that it prompted an air purifier company in China to use creative advertising titled "Breathe Again" to highlight this problem.[21] There is no doubt that the impact of climate change and pollution requires governments and city officials around the world to tackle the problems or face undesirable consequences. Singapore is no exception.

Besides the environment, despite the economic progress made globally, according to the World Bank latest report, there are still more than **700 million** people around the world in 2015 who live on less than USD1.90 a day (equivalent to USD1.25 a day in 2005 prices).[22]

Hence, being known globally as a city of excellence in many areas and as a regional hub for financial services (and wealth management), there are tremendous opportunities for stakeholders in Singapore to collaborate and tap on the huge global market to make cities green, sustainable and help alleviate poverty.

---

[19] http://www.channelnewsasia.com/news/singapore/unprecedented-low-levels/2025108.html

[20] http://www.straitstimes.com/singapore/environment/water-level-in-linggiu-reservoir-hits-record-low-continued-dry-spell-could

[21] https://www.youtube.com/watch?v=1e1qGc66W9k

[22] http://www.worldbank.org/en/news/press-release/2015/10/04/world-bank-forecasts-global-poverty-to-fall-below-10-for-first-time-major-hurdles-remain-in-goal-to-end-poverty-by-2030

Societal Gaps in the Continuum of Education

However, there are societal gaps which may prevent stakeholders in Singapore from tapping on such opportunities. Below are just a few:

1. **Lack of interest for environmental sustainability in our education system** — You may ask students (from primary school up to university level) in Singapore whether they would take up a Co-Curricular Activity (CCA) role in a Green Club or a career in environment-related studies, there is a high probability that less than one third would be interested.

2. **Low entrepreneurial drive among youths** — Having a good economy with jobs available for graduates has created a situation where youths today in Singapore do not see the need to venture into the high-risk path of entrepreneurship. The very low rate of start-ups among youths is thus not surprising.

3. **Relatively low level of volunteerism and involvement in community projects from the corporate sector** — With the needy communities being cared for over the years via government policies that are delivered via government agencies and non-profit organizations, the population at large has grown to expect this to continue.

Partly due to this, the majority of the business community today does not have a culture of sustained volunteerism and help towards community projects, unlike the pioneer generation.

Living in an increasingly globalized economy requires Singapore to consider doing more to help other countries, to make cities more sustainable, and also to help alleviate poverty.

An Incubation Hub for the Continuum of Youth Leadership Development

There are existing incubation hubs in Singapore today. However, not many would proactively reach out to the youth in numbers to guide them in career and youth development in a systematic manner. The Sustainability Place of Destiny (SPOD) aims to create an ecosystem to support the development of youth leaders from a young age, and incubate them to become social entrepreneurs over time.

Career Roadmap Development for Social Entrepreneurship

Not many people are born to be entrepreneurs and in Singapore, most would prefer a career as a professional working in an organization, whether in the public, private or people sector. Hence, the SPOD aims to assist our youths today to develop a career roadmap which will include social entrepreneurship, as depicted in the following figure.

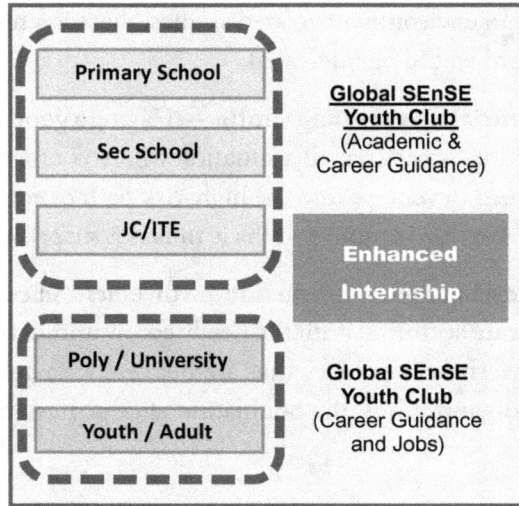

Career Roadmap on Social Entrepreneurship for the Youths

Hopefully, this will address some of the sustainability concerns listed earlier:

(1) **Educational roadmap for sustainability related to the environment and people** — The SPOD will collaborate with relevant partners to conduct workshop and facilitate projects to raise awareness of environmental sustainability and social entrepreneurship. These workshops will be aligned to the academic topics that the youths have learnt.

(2) **Hands-on approach towards social entrepreneurship** — This is merely an extension of the current Social Business Immersion Program (SBIP) which Global SEnSE (Social Entrepreneurship and Sustainable Ecosystem) currently conducts with AIESEC (a global youth-led non-profit), where exchange participants from over 120 countries would come to Singapore, be hosted by local students and get immersed into the social sector to learn best practices to support social causes, besides the youth leadership development for soft-skills like project management and effective life skills.

Engaging the Business Communities for Sustainable Future Cities

The Salvation Army Red Shield Industries Singapore was a signatory of the Memorandum of Understanding (MOU) for the Green and Sustainable Cities Initiative, spearheaded by Global SEnSE. The ultimate goal of this initiative is to encourage the development of a shared-value economy and to develop globally minded youth leaders.

The SPOD will help facilitate projects where the business communities will have the opportunities to be involved in community projects, whether by providing their products or services (at discounted rates or at no charge), or encouraging their employees to be involved.

An Integrated Approach for Student Projects and Internship

In order for projects to be done by students, it would be most effective if these projects are part of their typical student projects or internship. What we hope to do is to have the additional components of mentorship by professionals, as shown in the following figure. These mentors can do this as their CSR projects.

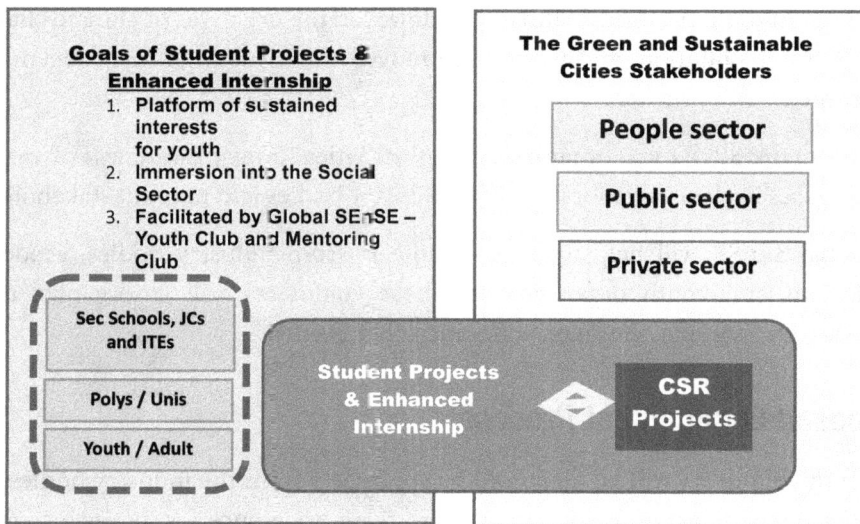

A Model for Student Projects and Enhanced Internship

Proposed Engagement Process

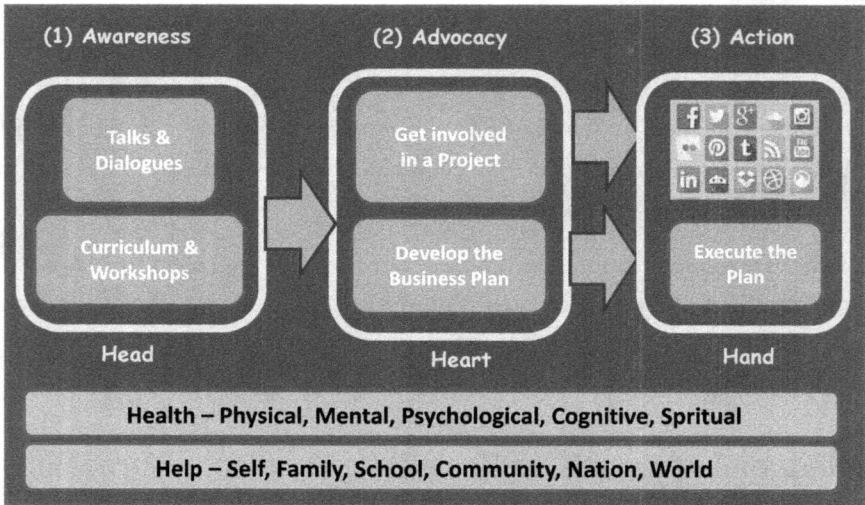

The Engagement Process of 3As (Awareness, Advocacy and Action) and 4Hs

Phase 1 — Awareness

The issue of environmental sustainability and community involvement does not rank high in our educational landscape. However, the negatives of climate change, air and water pollution, and waste have moved this issue high in the agenda of government policy makers.

Hence, the SPOD will organize various activities to raise awareness of various social causes in close collaboration with industry bodies and relevant stakeholders.

Global SEnSE will help manage volunteers from industry bodies, academic institutions and youth organizations. These volunteers will co-organize these activities, for example, seminars, talks and other events.

Proposed Engagement Process

Youth volunteers will be mentored by volunteers from the industry bodies and relevant stakeholders. These youths will be given preference for internship places and student projects.

Phase 2 — Advocacy

Once participants (corporates and youths) to the various awareness activities are keen to pursue further, they would be encouraged to conduct projects. This could be as simple as organizing an awareness campaign in their schools or companies or public places, as part of their respective Advocacy learning journeys.

For those who wish to develop entrepreneurship skills, then they will attend workshops to learn how to develop a Project or Business Plan.

Phase 3 — Action

As the saying goes, "Actions speak louder than words". Hence, the best way to learn is to do something. This is subject to one's own capability and ambition. It would be preferable to start small.

A critical and mandatory component is the **use of Social Media,** and participants are expected to leverage social media as part of their execution of their Project or Business Plan.

Conclusion

A common problem faced by the business world today is to figure out the next frontier and innovative business model to be sustainable. It is increasingly a globalized world, and the development of socially-minded youth leaders within the organization as described in this article is one approach to build the social capital of the organization.

43. Jump Start Self-Organizing

"It takes a village to raise a child."

Values Drive Us and the Organization

Like it or not, your underlying values govern your unconscious behaviors, like getting a drink, checking your email, checking for messages on Facebook or simply cutting your finger nails. Some people call it procrastination, but your value streams can be called "intentional-motivational state", which is part of a complex system that generates our affective tone, emotions or "form" of the day.

Thinking of our values as streams is a good analogy to understand this concept. Streams are continuously flowing and dynamic. Streams in a riverbed constantly change direction, speed, temperature and turbulence, constantly adjusting to the environment. Like the stream, our values adjust our inner feelings and our intensity of emotions change with the external environment.

Values shape our intentional-motivational state and they adjust to what is real in our experience. Your perceptions, experience and local interactions all play a part. It could be smooth as you driving your new car to work, but when a rock cracks your windshield, it could dramatically change the next moment. Your energy spikes, adrenalin rushes and a state of concentration changes. You focus on different sights, sounds and signs. For the rest of your day, all your interaction with others may change.

These effects may also affect others. We've all experienced being in a location where someone else is punished for doing something wrong. We may be walking into a room with a heated argument. It may not be targeted at us at all, but the energy affects us and may affect our value stream.

Value streams are complex, non-linear, chaotic flows of energy, which cannot be viewed simply as a system that can be modeled and managed. Every individual in a community or organization is complex and unique. A team cannot come to a rational solution that is based only on the "objective facts" of the matter, and no one can make a truly value-neutral, completely objective decision.

Viewing a community as a confluence of value streams and being able to feel "what is happening now" and "what is the current situation" is important in every ordinary and critical interaction in organizational life. The better the feel, the more responsive and more precise the conceptual abstractions we commonly use to represent organizational life. The impact can be different for two persons in the same situation, but nonetheless, they are real to each individual.

Although we relate to a community as a collection of value streams, we still acknowledge the fact that one event can impact individuals in different ways and to different extents.

Roles Form from Negotiating Values

Like all other species, people organize to distribute an energy load. It can be physical when we are lifting a heavy load or it may be cognitive when we come together to solve a puzzle. It can also be psychological when we share good news with each other. We come together and our value streams interact with each other, changing the flow. We "size up" the situation and "size up "one another, and this natural human process is called "self-organizing".

When we "size up" each other, we may discover the asymmetry of the relationship. When I want to push start a motorcycle, I may want to get the lightest person on the motorcycle while everyone else pushes the bike. Because of asymmetry in values, the power relationships are constantly negotiated and changed.

As we understand the shifting asymmetry between skill sets and value sets, we fall into our roles. The roles we play are from the organized interactions that we enter into in order to distribute the energy load required to fulfill our individual values. And these roles define the objectives that individuals need to perform to distribute the load.

The success of the organized performance depends upon fulfilling individual roles, which in turn depends upon maintaining sufficient relational stability or sustaining a threshold degree of coherence in the complex responsive processes operating at the level of the value-streams.

"Self-education is, I firmly believe, the only kind of education there is."
— Isaac Asimov

Self-organization

If we, the citizens of a society, think that it is important for people to be engaged and passionate about their work, and that they can all contribute to a better world, then we need to enable self-organization. Central planning and hierarchical decision-making are just too slow and ineffective for complex situations or changing conditions. In today's hyper connected world, people can navigate between different social networks, leverage on knowledge from different communities and crowdsource resources and solutions. It all hinges on individuals taking control of their learning, and organizations giving up control.

Understanding self-organization is based on knowing intention, identity and interaction. Intentional-motivational states are patterns that emerge through complex responsive processes operating in the value streams.

Identities form the continuous process as we negotiate asymmetrical values, skills and power relations. Roles form and the team is built on the interactions and orchestrated organization performances with individuals working towards their objective.

Self-organization is a major challenge for people who have been constantly told what to learn at school, and later, what to do at work.

The challenge in self-organizing processes is that we are not used to letting go of old identities and shape-shifting into new ones. The inertia is strong and people are uncomfortable in transition, where identities are not fixed or where fixed identities are challenged. People are obsessed with fixed roles, which represent the past conditions and context, and are unresponsive to the current or future conditions.

It is through the experience and learning that we grow up, and when we stop learning, we grow old.

— Robin Low

Shifting roles and forming new identities creates anxiety. Due to the organizational life around us, we live inside institutions where role-identities represent authoritarian and disciplinary power over us, and the inflexibility of the roles reflects the inflexible relations of institutionalized power. The challenge is to get the people with the right values into the right roles. Due to institutionalized asymmetry of power, many of the marginalized communities have anxieties when taking an important role as for many years, they have been living with self-doubt as the charity system and society "puts them in their place".

For effective self-organization, we need to design structures that allow flexible identities and creative roleplaying. These structures need to be human centric, adaptive and responsive to external changes and allow for a full spectrum of roles where anyone can participate. Role identities can evolve over time as skills and capacity grow, and it should respond to the needs and better distribute the load.

Self-organizing teams are much more flexible than hierarchical ones, but they require active and engaged members. One cannot cede power to the leader, because everyone is responsible for the leader they chose. Like democracy, self-organized teams are hard work. But they are best to deal with complexity. Hierarchies work well when information flows one down. They are good for command and control. They are handy to get things done in small groups. But hierarchies are rather useless to create, innovate, or change or to solve complex problems.

Trust and Transparency

One final piece to glue it all together is for the organization to have trust and transparency. The fundamental requirement for self-organizational teams is — trust. Trust is all about allowing what is most real, what is actually happening, what is actually the case, rather than what should be or is expected or demanded to be — to enter the public sphere so everyone can exercise their powers of discernment and practical judgment in a more informed and transparent way.

People working together require trust and transparency. You may limit interaction with rooms and desks, but you cannot control their internal thoughts. You may set up structures of disciplinary power, but you can never eliminate deviant thoughts.

The process of open participation means creating the conditions for "what is actually happening" to be able to be voiced in the shared spaces of conversation and interaction. People know what is relevant in the moment, even if they have trouble communicating it properly. The purpose of open participation is to allow the relevant content of what is actually happening to inform decision-making and responsive action taking. An honest response of how one feels about a decision often gets deeper to the root solution than a sound argument. Teams can learn how to trace their intuitions as well as their irritations, their enthusiasms as well as their fears, down to core operating values that make a difference.

When people build trust, they can endure the complex transition process where their roles and identities exist in a continuous flux, where individuals can reach their full potential and the teams can get the most out of their members. It takes time for people to break out of their "fixed roles" mentality and embrace the flux of creativity where roles and identities are shifting, but the community would be attending to what is real and building the capacity of each of the individuals in the community to accomplish the tasks.

As I often hear Carlos say, "it is not about picking the best team for the job, it is about making the best out of the team you have." Carlos believes in being inclusive and the fact that everyone can add value if given a chance.

44. Conscious Consumerism — The Needed Change

We stand with people we don't know, There are things we strive for we may not enjoy.

— Anonymous

Many people do question why they have to help others. "Why me? Can't you get a millionaire to support?"

Many other excuses include, "If they had worked hard and are pragmatic, they would not be like that," and "I've already donated last year for this cause."

We do not need to consider people who do not want to give. They will continue to have excuses. The change is needed for those who volunteer and donate on a regular basis, to make sure that their time and effort is spent to maximize social impact.

So what is this needed change?

It is not about giving and charity and giving, it is about redistribution and empowerment. Is what you are providing sustainable? And what will you achieve as the final goal in your actions? Will the community be better off after your actions?

It is not enough that you do nothing. Your going to bed with a clear conscience is not going to end people needing aid, your thinking climate change is terrible is not going to stop climate change. We need to accept that what hurts one of us hurts all of us. We need to get active; we need to hold ourselves and other people accountable. And we need to stop thinking that injustice in the world isn't to an extent our fault. Income inequality and the problems it brings are not going to solve themselves. We need to stop being a passive giver and start being active innovator.

Technology is on our side, but ...

When you think about the people with the power to change, the billionaires and the NGOs with funding, you would think that many of our social problems like income inequality and poverty would be greatly reduced.

Technology today is far more advanced and it even allows Carlos's one-year-old son, Guillermo, to stream his favorite videos on the tablet and play games. My niece would challenge my information with Google's aid at the age of six. With the connectivity of social media, you would assume a lot of the social injustices to be fixed.

I've seen Guillermo interact with my computer, touching the screen and attempting to swipe and click on icons, but as the monitor is not touch sensitive, he felt frustrated. I realized that it was exactly the same reaction I had when I was trying to work with traditional NGOs or foundations. When I tried to explain building communities and enabling technology to connect people together and solve problems, I did not get any buy in, but when I share these ideas with millennials, I can get overwhelming support.

I have heard the term "analog first generation", where people experience technology as it progresses, and "digital generation", the generation that grew up with fast internet and information on their smart products. This would apply to people and their mindsets as well.

People who are used to donations and aid will take time to adapt to the community empowerment concept. Just like emails, text messages on messaging platforms are slowly taking over informal conversations.

The problem we have today is that when people think about social innovation, it is still closely tied to legacy philosophies, processes and systems, which were crafted for a different era, which may have solved a different set of problems.

If you think billionaire philanthropists are coming to the rescue, think again.

The following excerpt is from an article on the "Ultra-Rich 'Philanthrocapitalist' Class" by Common Dreams, a non-profit independent newscenter.[23]

> Looking at agriculture and farming, meanwhile, the Gates Foundation is undermining self-determination and local solutions in measurable ways.
> "The vast majority of the Gates Foundation's agricultural development grants focus on Africa," the report notes. "However, over 80 percent of the U.S. $669 million to NGOs went to organizations based in the U.S. and Europe, with only 4 percent going to Africa-based NGOs. Similarly, of the U.S. $678 million

---

[23] http://www.commondreams.org/news/2016/01/15/ultra-rich-philanthrocapitalist-class-undermining-global-democracy-report

grants to universities and research centers, 79 percent went to grantees in the U.S. and Europe and only 12 percent to recipients in Africa."

Both the Gates and Rockefeller Foundations have been slammed by international grassroots groups, including the global peasant movement La Via Campesina, for their international role in exporting big agricultural models, privatizing food policies, and expanding the power of companies like Monsanto.

Facebook is going out of its way to emphasize that CEO Mark Zuckerberg's pledge to give away 99% of his company shares is not about charity, but philanthropy.

The initiative that will receive the charity, the Chan Zuckerberg Initiative, is set up as an LLC (Limited Liability Company), not as a charitable trust. This means that the LLC can do whatever it wants, including private investments generating profits. And yes, it can retain its profits and not give it to charity.

While charity will certainly be one of the profit's destinations, it is far from being the only one. The money according to a Facebook SEC (Securities and Exchange Commission) filing, will go to "philanthropic, public advocacy, and other activities for the public good."

If you think Mark Zuckerberg is giving up 99% of his US$45 billion to charity, you are wrong. Many rich people have annouced this, and let me explain why. It is most likely not out of the kindness of their hearts or altruism, but rather, because it makes economic sense.

(1) Paying less tax.

This is a troubling trend and most of the rich do not pay a high percentage of their salaries as tax. And yes, if Mark Zuckerberg puts his money into this initiative, 99% of the money will not qualify for capital gains tax.

So in simple terms, **Mark Zuckerberg will transfer ownership of his Facebook stock without paying capital gains taxes.** His children will also have everything, untouched by estate taxes.

(2) It is an LLC.

As an LLC, he can invest any way he wants. He can use SOME profits to focus on his philanthropic goals, but most of it to generate more profits. Not a bad thing actually as the more money it acquires, the more it can be used for philanthropic purposes, but it is not primarily for philanthropic goals as it is not setup as a charitable trust.

"The Chan Zuckerberg Initiative will pursue its mission by funding non-profit organizations, making private investments and participating in policy debates, in each case with the goal of generating positive impact in areas of great need," it (a Facebook release) said. *"Any profits from investments in companies will be used to fund additional work to advance the mission."* (BuzzFeed)

(3) This is not happening immediately.

The Facebook founder is not giving away 99% of his Facebook shares all at once. He will be doing it over the course of his life.

(4) Moving money to his own organization.

Rather than give to existing nonprofits, business leaders are increasingly siphoning their fortune into their own organizations.[24]

(5) Facebook does not need tax benefits.

With this move, Zuckerberg no longer needs to depend on tax benefits, he is able to give up his stocks, pay less taxes and remain in power of his company.

So is this a good or bad thing?

It is too early to tell, but you can be sure that this is a smart thing for anyone who is rich to do.

Business success does not equate to philanthropic expertise. "Just because you were successful in the for-profit world doesn't mean that nonprofits are a bunch of bleeding-heart idiots that need you to come in and show them how it's done," said Ken Berger, the managing director of the social-good data service Algorhythm.

---

[24] http://www.huffingtonpost.com/entry/zuckerberg-donation_us_565e385ae4b079b2818c770d?adsSite Override=in&section=india

45. Iteration versus Innovation

Innovation is a new idea, or a more effective device or process. Innovation can be viewed as the application of better solutions that meet new requirements, unarticulated needs, or existing market needs.

Iteration is the act of repeating a process, either to generate an unbounded sequence of outcomes, or with the aim of approaching a desired goal, target or result. Each repetition of the process is also called "iteration" and the results from one iteration are used as the starting point for the next iteration.

When I talk about social innovation, I'm not talking about social iteration, but social innovation, which is about change and disruption. If past attempts have not found a solution to the problem, repetition with minor changes is not going to solve the problems.

The fact that some old NGOs still exist without adapting to the times is truly amazing, and perhaps unlike with companies, market forces apply less and many people still do not understand the new paradigm of community empowerment or social business.

Sometimes when people think about iteration versus innovation, it may feel like an "either or" choice, but in reality, they work hand in hand. Let me clarify some misconceptions:

Innovation is Expensive

There are no correlations between innovation and R&D spending. Through consultations with companies, I realized that many of the innovative companies have innovation as part of their corporate culture.

Innovation is Disruption

A lot of innovation starts with small scale prototypes and incremental change. A lot of market leaders are early adopters of lean principles and they constantly adjust and adapt to the current conditions. Innovation may lead to a disruption eventually, but it is not as fast as it sounds.

First Mover has the Advantage

Trying to create the first solution to a problem which is unsolved is usually not easy. More often than not, we see pioneers of an idea or product blown away by companies that are second and third in line. However, in the case of social innovation, once you build trust with a community, you do have an advantage over others trying to work with the community. It is not, however, a winner-takes-all game. More solutions and support are always welcomed.

You Must Innovate All the Time

Broader industry trends and developments — new regulations, or the emergence of new technologies — also need to be taken into account when determining whether it's time to innovate. A good approach to innovation is not doing all at once, it is iterative and continuous.

Innovation usually happens when the time is right. When new renewable energy is more efficient and costs less, it may be time to power villages off the grid with solar energy.

46. Social Innovation is Not an Easy Task

The people you engage with may not be pleasant or grateful. Your friends and family may turn on you, and others in society may question your motivations or sanity.

I've met with some people running a grocery co-operative in San Francisco near a homeless encampment. Initially, the customers and workers in the co-operative were very supportive, giving the homeless food and supplies.

But as the encampment grew, and as there are no public restrooms and showers in the area, the restroom in the co-operative was left with messes of feces, urine or vomit. The co-operative is also seeing an increase in theft, violent encounters and mental health issues in and around the store. It's common to see individuals enter the store yelling or getting physical, or exposing themselves to patrons outside the store.

After the muggings of some shoppers, many shoppers are taking their business elsewhere, fearing for their safety. There is not much support from the local government, and volunteers who started a community ambassador program to talk to the homeless people weekly are discouraged as the program has been poorly received.

With public resentment, the work can be even more overwhelming as business is affected, numbers of homeless people are increasing, and the neighborhood is getting worse. The support you get from volunteers is dwindling.

Just like a story, there are always ups and downs in a project. As part of the journey, there are tests and challenges where you learn and gain experience from the interaction. However, there may be no happy ending. The community you are supporting may not even acknowledge your existence.

Like in life, you win some and you lose some. You may come across a solution to reduce poverty and empower many people, giving them hope and options. You get to test your perseverance and patience, creativity and adaptability. You may put in countless hours and suddenly realize that the community is just taking you for granted, and the project cannot continue without you driving it, and the community does not want to take accountability for their actions.

What I often learn is the perspective and views from marginalized communities. I often get inspired by their innovative solutions created with limited resources, which I can apply to my businesses or share with communities in other locations.

Engaging with many different communities also made me realize that communities are capable of solving problems by themselves, and sometimes with a little support. But external organizations may bring their own solutions to destroy what the communities created without engagement.

I have learnt that my approach to everything I do now — taking them as learning experiences — opens my mind to learn more, do more and achieve more. It is not about helping people; it is about creating options and testing ideas. Whether it succeeds or fails, treat it as a learning experience where you get better at what you do, and learn from failures and examine what went wrong.

Everyone has a role to play in the community, and in most cases, ignoring the problem or expecting someone else to do it does not make the issue go away. There are opportunities in everything, and it does take time and effort to understand the root cause of the problem and try different solutions to solve it.

> *The most important question to ask is, is it about looking good or is it about living good? How wonderful you feel within yourself is more important than how wonderful you look. If you are really feeling wonderful, everybody will feel wonderful in your presence. If you are blissed out, everybody who comes in touch with you, one way or the other, will begin to experience that bliss.*
>
> *If you feel frustrated or nasty, if someone comes up to you, you tend to be nasty to that person. Don't try to control your behavior, no morals, no ethics, you just manage your interiority. If you keep a joyful blissful state, you are guaranteed to be a wonderful human being and you will build a wonderful society. What you eventually do, does not depend on your values, but simply because of your humanity. Only humanity is guaranteed, as some people will always find ways around morality.*
>
> *— Sadhguru*

If you are planning to make an impact in the world, that impact will happen because of your intensity and substance, not just because of the arrangement of your appearance and the money in your bank account.

47. Responsibility & Reciprocity

I do feel that this may be a secret ingredient in sustainability which is much needed in a good social project. I've seen many successful social innovations, and often ask this question, why is this not succeeding everywhere? And one of the simple reasons — scale.

It is sometimes not easy to scale up, and finding more funds or people who can help with the training may be tough. However, not a lot of people have actually asked, how about getting the recipients of the training or aid to help?

The term "paying it forward" is an expression for describing the beneficiary of a good deed repaying it to others instead of to the original benefactor. This concept is not new, and can be applied to far more organizations.

The idea of getting the recipients of aid to contribute and support someone else has a lot of benefits. Firstly, it reduces the resources needed to benefit someone else in a similar situation. For example, if a person who could not afford to get to college gets a scholarship, that person could pay it forward and sponsor someone else to go to college once they come out and get their job.

Secondly, it gives the recipient hope — hope that they can also succeed in the program because someone who has already benefitted from it is supporting them. I've seen many of these programs, and in Boston, Haley House has a program that is a transitional training program that strives to break the cycle of incarceration by supporting men and women returning home to the community. Upon the completion of training and getting a job, the recipients of the training have to train others coming in and support the community. The new recipients have a role model to look up to who was in their position a few months ago, and who has now successfully completed the training and gained employment.

Next, it makes the original recipient of the aid appreciate what they received more, because they have to give to others whom they were once like. Giving allows you to break free from the feeling of guilt, and shows abundance. A person feels more empowered when they are in a position to help others. They appreciate it more because the aid is "not free".

There is also continuity and sustainability. If you have a system where people receiving support have to support others, you will have a system that can repeat and continue to give. For a successful system, if one recipient can help two or more other people that are disadvantaged like they were previously, then there can be a multiplier effect which can benefit far more people in the long run. It will also be sustainable as the system can be continuous.

Giving the recipients of aid and training a responsibility to help others is giving them a sense of hope and purpose. It does make them want to do more and the sense of purpose can motivate them to try harder in order to succeed and help others. Communities are strong when individuals inside care about others and want to support one another instead of competing with one another just to win and put others down.

Poverty is a complex problem that just one solution can never fix. Just like fixing a car after flood damage, changing the engine alone does not make the car run fine again. For many years, we have tried to solve the gaps of society by donating to charities and volunteering. However, the number of people living in poverty just seems to increase.

It is not that the aid is not required by these communities. Aid and welfare are just temporary solutions, and when they are applied long term, dependencies may be created. With the widening income gap and increasing frequency of natural and man-made disasters, we need new solutions to solve the pressing problems. Together with technology and social media, we can accomplish today much more than what we could years ago.

I believe many of the solutions to the problems we see can be found within the community itself. The community members are the ones who have experienced the problems first hand and who have local knowledge. Following the principles of Never Help; Engage, Enable, Empower & Connect, crowdsourced solutions which leverage on collective intelligence will hopefully bring out bold disruptive ideas, challenging the norms and bringing about sustainable change.

#ImpactJourney[25]

Our awareness of humans belonging to different cultures and beliefs can be transformed in a positive way through direct contact and conversation with even one member of that group. For this reason, we do webinars and LivingBridgesPlanet talks together. The proactive commitment, fun and mutual support is here alive in the fb groups, webinars, conversations on- and offline.

Change makers in such activities understand that they are not alone in their problems. They can get courage from the example of other change makers, learning and striving to overcome their own challenges. In turn, the example of your own journey can powerfully trigger courage in others. You are welcome to bring your own community in.

Support each other! When we al engage in open dialogue, in our own ways, the world begins to shine in a warmer, more human light. We belief that dialogue is absolutely essential if we are to build a world in which no one is left behind.

#open #random #supportive

[25] Impact Journey is an outgrowth of Living Bridges Planet, a global facilitator network inspired by strength-based and social capital approaches to enable change. https://www.facebook.com/groups/ImpactJourney/

48. Conclusion

Helping is complicated and easy to mess up. That much is obvious now at the end of this book. But this does not mean it is ok to not try. Doing nothing at all is not a good option.

The problem with helping is that for the most part, it involves people being too assured of their ways to learn to do things differently and instead, just following status quo. There needs to be a better understanding of the problem, and purer motivations, with less religious ideology and more economics. But much condescension from colonizing countries towards the formerly colonized and sometimes, a racist mindset, may make people think otherwise.

"There is nothing small or insufficient about what they do, except, that is, in the tragic human sense that all effort is insufficient, all glory transient, all solutions inadequate to the challenge, all aid insufficient to the need"

— *David Rieff, in* A Bed for the Night: Humanitarianism in Crisis

I have often been in a position where I question myself: how am I going to change other people when I don't exactly understand what is going on myself? What people tell you is usually not their immediate problem, because the problem is too complicated for someone external to understand immediately. They tell you what you want to hear and so they can get what they expect to get.

Change is difficult. Most people are difficult to change, and they sometimes do, but slowly and only slightly. They are not always grateful — some are resentful instead. Being too emotionally involved clouds judgement. On days when one is confronted with a devastating problem that cannot be fixed, the misery and helplessness rub off, perhaps making one feel angry and blaming systems and society for what one cannot fix.

Being angry does not solve the problem. Resilience is important and one needs to be tough, but not detached. Optimism, coupled with creativity and innovation may be a way to continuously look for solutions when encountering a dead end. Complaining does not help; only when the solution is found is the problem solved.

"If you insist on working with the poor, if this is your vocation, then at least work among the poor who can tell you to go to hell. It is incredibly unfair for you to impose

yourselves on a village where you are so linguistically deaf and dumb that you don't even understand what you are doing, or what people think of you. And it is profoundly damaging to yourselves when you define something that you want to do as "good", a "sacrifice" and "help" … I am here to challenge you to recognize your inability, your powerlessness and your incapacity to do the "good" which you intended to do."

— *Ivan Illich, 1968*

Appendix

Platforms for Supporting Next Generation Businesses and Resilient Societies

http://aseanregionalforum.asean.org/http://neighborhoodeconomics.org/http://www.ogunte.com — Women-focused

http://www.socentix.com

http://www.volans.com/volans/

http://www.tallbergfoundation.org/

http://bayarea.impacthub.net/

http://www.ideasproject.eu/IDEAS_wordpress/deliverables/index.html

http://www.unconvention.co.in/

http://www.facebook.com/pages/Social-Bancorp/183421055082853

http://groaction.com/

http://www.facebook.com/pages/GroAction/215195255184778?sk=app_208195102528120

http://www.joyliving.net

http://www.impacthub.net/http://mentorcapitalnet.org/

https://www.facebook.com/pages/Call-to-Change/159881987362799

http://www.sitawi.net/

http://www.globalgiving.org/projects/sitawi-loan-fund-for-social-enterprises-in-brazil

http://www.socialcapitalmarkets.net

http://www.relief20.com

http://www.globalsustainabilityjam.org/

http://www.globalservicejam.org/

http://www.openworld.com/

https://www.makesense.org/

http://mindtimemaps.com

http://mindtime.com

http://collabcafewelly.tumblr.com

http://nationbuilder.com/

http://www.socialenterpriseeurope.co.uk/

http://techaloo.com/

http://www.socialenterprise-chicago.org

http://www.facebook.com/ecoNVERGE

http://www.relayfoundation.org

https://www.facebook.com/OpenCSR/http://www.goodfornothing.com/how-it-works

http://www.opportunejobs.com

http://www.p-ced.com

http://www.youtube.com/TheRationalFuture

http://www.i-open.org/

http://civ.do/

http://www.co-society.com/about/our-story/

https://www.kl.nl/en/

http://bundlr.com/b/education3

http://incentivize.us/

http://p2pfoundation.net/

http://www.facebook.com/Nationalyoungwomenscouncil

http://www.jci.cc/

http://www.harva.co.in/

http://www.gramweb.net/

http://www.collectiveself.com/frequently-asked-questions/what-is-a-friendship-incubator/

http://www.blue-planet-life.org/en/welcome.html

http://globalimpactcollective.org/

http://www.leadersinstitute.com.au/

http://www.rehan.com/

http://www.idec2013.org/ — International Democratic Education Conference

http://www.mediapoint.md/

http://greensmyles.com/

http://www.bagosphere.com/

http://shapeshifters.net/

http://educar.org/

http://www.communityled.co.za/

http://www.lgtvp.com/

http://www.azimpremjifoundation.org/

http://www.facebook.com/groups/smallisgreat/

http://jom.sagepub.com/content/early/2016/02/25/0149206316633268.full

http://www.facebook.com/groups/sosialentreprenor/

http://dreamups.org/

http://producism.org/

http://metacurrency.org/

http://www.ingenesist.com/

http://www.arthaplatform.com/

http://www.eq-cap.com/

http://www.livingmandala.com/Living_Mandala/Living_Mandala.html

http://maximpact.com/

http://reconomy.net/

http://www.akhuwat.org.pk/

https://www.coursera.org/

http://www.iachievegroup.com/

http://pashafund.com/

http://www.fsg.org/

http://www.womensweb.in/articles/women-entrepreneurs-in-india/

http://about.me/reachscale.com

http://www.thecitizensmedia.com/

http://www.selco-india.com/

http://www.coolmeia.org/

http://www.molequedeideias.net/

http://www.silo.is/3x11/

http://www.facebook.com/SliceBizhttp://www.buckybox.com/

http://www.societal-innovation.org/

http://createachangenow.org/

http://defindia.net/

http://thealternative.in/

http://www.dreamitventures.com/

http://www.svx.ca/

http://www.techpear.com/

https://www.asiaforgood.com/

Movements/Social Change

http://jellyweek.tumblr.com/

http://www.facebook.com/pages/Call-to-Change

http://www.uterus-myomatosus.net

http://www.WishesWell.com/

http://www.bankofideas.org.uk/

http://socialforesight.net

http://scwf12.wordpress.com http://www.yesworld.org/

http://seedfreedom.in/
http://www.facebook.com/pages/YUVA-Foundation
https://www.facebook.com/groups/SOCAP/
http://www.partnershipforchange.net/
http://www.icaf.org/ and http://www.facebook.com/ICAF.org — The arts for the development of creativity and empathy
http://www.thinkimpact.com/
http://changeinc.tigweb.org/
http://www.sekem.com/
http://www.peers.org/

Social Ventures/Social Enterprises/Social Businesses

http://williamjamesfoundation.org/
http://www.nesta.org.uk/
http://www.fairtravel.com/
http://www.idea.com.gr/ and http://www.idea.com.gr/i_landing_page.html
http://globaler-wandel.blogspot.com/2011/11/barcamp-how-internet-changes-our.html
https://www.facebook.com/pages/Call-to-Change
http://www.betterworldbooks.com
http://www.makechange.tv/
http://www.treeswaterpeople.org/
http://www.intolife.no/
http://www.terracycle.net/en-US/
http://www.socentlab.com/
http://www.buckybox.com/
http://www.firstpowercanada.ca/
http://www.enspiral.com
http://www.purpose.com
http://www.luontoportti.com/suomi/en/
http://www.facebook.com/eco-sTrEAMs (@ eco-sTrEAMs)
http://www.facebook.com/eco.ViVaCity (@ eco-ViVaCity)
http://www.facebook.com/eco.Nable (@ eco-Nable)
http://www.facebook.com/groups/econologics/ (@ ECONOLOGICS — Incisive)
http://www.digitalgreen.org/farmerbook/
http://laplandvuollerim.se/en/
http://haleyhouse.org/

Knowledge Converged

http://www.veggbox.appspot.com/
http://ideasociety.com/
http://www.advancednrgsolutions.com/
http://www.p-ced.com
http://www.facebook.com/pages/Aangan/176857645688413
http://www.youtube.com/watch?v=Mwi4d4mCUNk&feature=youtu.be
http://www.mothercourage.no/
http://www.openideo.com/
http://www.laplandvuollerim.se/

Funds/Financing

http://www.bonventure.de/en/home.html (only German speaking regions)
http://www.vilcap.com — Village capital seed funding network for the research programme SOCENT
http://www.toniic.com — Global impact investment angel network
http://inventure.no/
http://www.fordfoundation.org/Grants/
https://www.opensocietyfoundations.org
 http://www.asef.org — Asia-Europe Foundation
http://givkwik.com/

Inspiration/Strategy

http://www.blueoceanstrategy.com/ — Making competition irrelevant
http://foundups.com/ — Changing the world together
http://100startup.com/tour/ — Build a Startup with $100, keep it lean
http://steveblank.com/ — Steve Blank is a teacher for entrepreneurship
http://projectofhow.com/ — Open library of creative methods
http://www.cultural-entrepreneurship-institute.de/en/ — Theoretical wisdom for the Global Society
http://www.respectserendipity.com — Serendipity as the ultimate source of inspiration
http://www.differentoffice.com — Stories of self-created, soul-satisfying work spaces
http://www.methodkit.com/ — Cards decks for defining startups, sustainable development and gender equality

Inspirational Blogs

http://www.asmundseip.com/
http://truemaisha.blogspot.se/?spref=fb
http://hildygottlieb.com/
http://www.doing.gd/
http://sharedtracks.wordpress.com/

Text/Knowledge/Books

http://en.wikipedia.org/wiki/Impact_investing
http://www.facebook.com/piceberlin — Spreading knowledge for cultural return
http://www.enablingcity.com

Causes of War and Peace

https://www.theobjectivestandard.com/2014/10/causes-war-peace/

Countries Do Get Happier When They Get Richer — But Only If They Share The Wealth

http://www.fastcoexist.com/3055098/countries-do-get-happier-when-they-get-richer-but-only-if-they-share-the-wealth

Today, we stand with people we don't know. There are things we strive for that we may not enjoy.

Miracles belong to storybooks; being outraged does not solve problems.

To create the future we want, we must take action; Have the courage to try ideas — big or small; Learn from our failures, accept criticism; Have patience, be inclusive; And believe that there is always a solution as long as we put in the effort.

Because we are all humans living on the same planet.

www.ingramcontent.com/pod-product-compliance
Lightning Source LLC
Chambersburg PA
CBHW070336270326
41926CB00017B/3893